THE CATHOLIC UNIVERSITY OF AMERICA
CANON LAW STUDIES
No. 204

THE UNION OF PARISHES

AN HISTORICAL SYNOPSIS AND COMMENTARY

BY

REV. THOMAS M. MUNDY, A.B., S.T.L., J.C.L.

Priest of the Archdiocese of Philadelphia

A DISSERTATION

Submitted to the Faculty of the School of Canon Law of the Catholic University of America in Partial Fulfillment of the Requirements for the Degree of Doctor of Canon Law

THE CATHOLIC UNIVERSITY OF AMERICA PRESS, INC.
WASHINGTON, D. C.
1945

Nihil Obstat:

EDUARDUS ROELKER, S.T.D., J.C.D.,
Censor Deputatus

Washingtonii, D. C., die XV Maii, 1944

Imprimatur:

✠ D. CARD. DOUGHERTY,
Archiepiscopus Philadelphiensis

Philadelphiae, die XVII Maii, 1944

The Walther Printing House
Philadelphia, Pennsylvania

TO MY

PARENTS

TABLE OF CONTENTS

CHAPTER IV

CHAPTER V

FOREWORD

The parish is to the Church what the family is, or at least should be, to a sovereign State, that is to say, it is its fundamental unit of government and organization. From no other single ecclesiastical institute, perhaps, more than from the parish has the Church derived its essential note of unity in disciplinary matters. Fully aware of the benefits that have been derived from parochial organization, the Church has long since commanded that parishes be erected in all countries subject to its common law. Even in mission countries, where full organization has not as yet been realized, quasi-parishes are to be established at the earliest opportune moment.[1]

It would, indeed, be ideal if all parishes could remain in the state in which they were originally founded. It must be remembered, however, that they have to do with the government of human beings. Accordingly, the legislation which governs parishes must be equipped to share the vicissitudes that are an inevitable part of human life. These vicissitudes in the lives of parishioners often compel a corresponding change in the original status of the parish. The change in parishes may take place by way of a change of site, a division, a dismemberment, a transmutation, a suppression, or a union. It is with the last of these types of modification that the pages of this dissertation will be concerned.

Were this work concerned with the treatment of an entire ecclesiastical institute it might be preferable to separate the historical section from the canonical commentary. The truth of the matter is, however, that the subject under consideration treats of but one aspect of that institute known as a parish. Historical data are but fragmentary, and the legislation, for the most part introduced by the Council of Trent, once established remained unchanged up until the Code of Canon Law. It scarcely lends itself, therefore, to forming a separate, logical section of this work. Wherefore it has been deemed advisable to incorporate pre-Code legislation with the commentary on the law of the Code. Wherever possible, the writer has explained pre-Code legislation before proceeding with the canonical commentary.

1 Canon 216, §1, §2.

An entire chapter has been devoted to comparing the elements of a canonical parish with those of an ecclesiastical benefice, and the conclusion is demonstrated that the parish is an ecclesiastical benefice. This conclusion, it is true, while justifiable, may appear as trite and one which no longer requires proof. The writer feels, however, that it affords the necessary foundation for the investigation to be made in these pages. Throughout the entire work the words *benefice* and *parish* are employed interchangeably. Moreover, though the Code does contain special legislation concerning the union of parishes in particular, it also contains legislation concerning the union of benefices in general, which legislation must be explored if the commentary is to be complete. It has seemed necessary, therefore, to establish from the very outset the fact that a canonical parish is an ecclesiastical benefice.

The writer is well aware of the fact that unions of parishes are, in practice, more the exception than they are the rule. Their importance must not, therefore, be overemphasized. And yet, it may well be that the day is not far off when they will be employed more frequently. The present war has brought with it changes in all spheres of life. The ecclesiastical sphere is no exception. Because of the influx of people into certain localities for the sake of war-time employment, new settlements, and therefore, new parishes have sprung up almost over night. It is to be doubted whether they will endure after the struggle has been terminated. It would seem then that they may give cause for their union with some other established parish. Again, this migration of people into the larger cities is, in many small parishes, occasioning an alarming decrease in the number of parishioners, and the problem for pastor and bishop alike as to how to continue to support these depleted parishes is daily becoming increasingly more difficult. It may well be that ultimately some of these parishes will have to be united among themselves.

Finally, the writer takes occasion to express his gratitude to His Eminence, Dennis Cardinal Dougherty, Archbishop of Philadelphia, for the opportunity of advanced studies; to the Faculty of the School of Canon Law of the Catholic University of America; and to all others who have in any way, by interest and by active aid, contributed towards the realization of this dissertation.

CHAPTER I

PRELIMINARY NOTIONS

The specific purpose of this work is to study in detail the canonical norms governing the union of parishes. The Code of Canon Law treats of this matter in canons 1419-1428. Before entering upon a particular consideration of the matter at hand, however, the writer has deemed it advisable to furnish briefly some general preliminary notions.

In the first place, since *parishes* are under consideration, it appears indicated here to give some idea of the etymology of the word itself. Secondly, parishes were not an essential part of ecclesiastical organization from the very beginning of the Church; they are rather a product of the evolution of ecclesiastical legislation and of the Church itself, brought into being both by expediency and by necessity. Hence, it will be fitting to give a brief resumé of the historical development of the institute. Let it be stated at the very outset, however, that the writer makes no pretension whatsoever of giving a detailed and intricate study of the history of parishes. To do so, for his purpose, would be both superfluous and entirely unnecessary; superfluous, because it does not form an essential part of this work; unnecessary, because other writers have already completed the task.[1]

The third point for consideration will be to determine just what is meant by a parish according to the Code of Canon Law.

1 For a more complete discussion of the history of parishes one can consult with profit: Bouix (1808-1870), *Tractatus de Parocho* (Parisiis, 1855), pp. 16-43; Rossi, *De Paroecia* (Romae: Pustet, 1923), p. 1; Bastnagel, *The Appointment of Parochial Adjutants and Assistants*, The Catholic University of America Canon Law Studies, n. 58 (Washington, D. C.: The Catholic University of America, 1930), pp. 3-22; Coady, *The Appointment of Pastors*, The Catholic University of America Canon Law Studies, n. 52 (Washington, D. C.: The Catholic University of America, 1929), pp. 4-14, 29; Connolly, *The Canonical Erection of Parishes*, The Catholic University of America Canon Law Studies, n. 114 (Washington, D. C.: The Catholic University of America, 1938), pp. 12-41.

Finally, the union of parishes constitutes a *modification* in the benefice. A *modification* is any alteration in the benefice which affects the condition in which it was when originally erected. There are various modes of modification possible in a benefice, namely: union, change of site, division, dismemberment, transmutation, and suppression. The Code itself explains what is to be understood by these terms.[2] For a clear understanding of the subject to be treated, and in order to avoid any misunderstanding, it will, therefore, be helpful to give from the very outset a precise idea of each of the various forms of modification.

Article 1. The Etymology of the Term "Parish"

Practically all canonists are in agreement in deriving the word *paroecia* from the Greek παροικία (παροικέω: to live near, or to live at), and understand by the term *a place of habitation.*[3] The use of the word *paroecia* dates back to the very beginning of Christianity, as evidenced by its appearance in the earliest ecclesiastical documents. Thus, by way of example, the Church of Smyrna in the middle of the second century addressed itself to the *parishes* of the Catholic Church throughout the world.[4] Obviously, the word is intended here to signify an entire diocese, since at that time there was no such thing as a parish in our modern sense of the word.

Consequently, although it can safely be stated that the word was in use from the earliest times, nonetheless it was most certainly not accepted in those times in the same sense in which it

[2] *Codex Iuris Canonici Pii X Pontificis Maximi iussu digestus Benedicti Papae XV auctoritate promulgatus* (Romae: Typis Polyglottis Vaticanis, 1917. Reimpressio, 1936), canons 1419, 1421. Hereafter to be referred to by simply citing the canon and its number.

[3] For a more complete study of the etymology, cf. Wernz (1842-1914), *Ius Decretalium* (3. ed., 6 vols., Prati, 1913-1914), II, n. 821, footnote 6; Bouix, *De Parocho*, pp. 5-12; Rossi, *De Paroecia*, n. 1; Coady, *The Appointment of Pastors*, pp. 1-3.

[4] Migne (1800-1875), *Patrologiae Cursus Completus, Series Graeca* (161 vols., Parisiis, 1856-1866), V, 1029; Journel, *Enchiridion Patristicum* (Friburgi Brisgoviae: Herder and Co., 1937), n. 77.

is understood today. In the rural districts up until about the sixth century, and in the cities until about the twelfth century, the word was used to signify an entire diocese, that is, the whole territory of some particular bishop.[5] After the Council of Trent (1545-1563), however, the word *paroecia* came more and more clearly to be accepted in its present signification, so that long before the Code of Canon Law it had already the precise meaning attributed to it today in the Code.[6]

Article 2. The Historical Development of Parishes

The system of parochial organization within the Catholic Church has long been the object of envy and of admiration. Apart from matters of faith and morals, no other single factor within the entire Church has perhaps lent itself as readily for adaptation among such a variety of peoples, customs, and circumstances as that institute known as the parish. It is based upon man's natural instinct for association and organization. Yet, it would be a gross mistake to believe that full parochial organization was the state of affairs from the inception of the Church. It was not until after the lapse of centuries that the system acquired that state of quasi-perfection which can be observed today.

There were some who went so far as to maintain that the office of pastor, and therefore the institute of the parish itself, were of divine constitution. According to this opinion, pastors are the successors of the seventy-two disciples, just as bishops are the successors of the twelve Apostles.[7] Historically, however, it is certain that up until, at the very least, the fourth century no such institute as the parish was to be found.[8]

5 For evidence of the word in this sense throughout the various centuries, cf. Bouix, *De Parocho*, pp. 7-12.

6 Canon 216, § 1.

7 For a discussion of this erroneous opinion, cf. Bouix, *De Parocho*, pp. 45-75; Maroto (1875-1937), *Institutiones Iuris Canonici* (2 vols., Matriti, 1919), II, 97.

8 Thomassinus (1619-1695), *Vetus et Nova Ecclesiae Disciplina* (3 vols., Parisiis, 1688), pars I, lib. II, cap. XXI, n. 2; Devoti (1744-1820), *Institutionum Canonicarum Libri IV* (4 vols., ed. septima Romana, Romae,

The lack of parishes in the early centuries should not occasion any undue wonder. The Church was just beginning. The early disciples were concerned more with the substance of Christianity than with the external forms of discipline which it was destined to assume. When, therefore, the Apostles first converted a city, their only preoccupation was to find some neophyte upon whom they might impose hands that he in turn might govern those of the same city who followed him into the Christian fold.

An episcopal cathedral was established, humble though it may have been, and this alone served as the center of worship. Indeed, it was a matter of law in the early Church that all liturgical functions were reserved to the bishop, either personally, or through some priest whom he selected to function in his stead.[9] Anyone attempting to transgress against this spirit of unity was condemned.[10] The priests and deacons assisted the bishop in the care of souls, but at no time in the early centuries did they rule a determined group in their own name. When their services were required it was generally for one particular function *(ad actum tantum)*. True, they may at times have supplied the place of the bishop in the rural districts habitually *(ad modum habitus)*, but in such a case their ministry was entirely dependent upon the will of the bishop, so that no certain priest had a stable rule over any particular group of the faithful.[11]

After the persecutions and the Edict of Constantine (313), the number of the faithful increased so that it became impossible for the bishop alone to govern directly the souls entrusted to his care. Moreover, whereas originally the first Christian communities had been confined to the cities, there were now large numbers of Christians in the outlying or rural districts. Originally, when they were but few in number, these Christians had come into the

1829), lib. I, tit. III, sect. 10; Bouix, *De Parocho*, pp. 16, 22; Maroto, *Institutiones Iuris Canonici*, II, n. 762.

9 Cf. Bouix, *De Parocho*, p. 17.

10 Bastnagel, *Appointment of Parochial Adjutants and Assistants*, p. 12.

11 Ferraris (+ ca. 1763), *Bibliotheca Canonica Iuridica Moralis Theologica necnon Ascetica Polemica Rubristica Historica* (9 vols., Romae, 1885-1899), V. "parochia", n. 7.

cities to participate in the divine services. Now, however, because of the increase in their number and the inconveniences created by the distances which separated them from the cities, it became necessary to abandon the ancient sense of direct contact between the bishop and his flock. The Christians in the rural districts were then entrusted to priests who remained permanently in their midst. In this innovation the beginning of our modern parochial system is to be found.

It is still difficult to determine with accuracy just when this system of parochial organization began. It is definitely known that the change first took place in the East, and some time later in the West. It can, however, be stated with comparative safety that the inception of parish life in the rural districts dates back to about the fourth century, although the name *parish* was not applied to these rural districts until about the sixth century.

In the cities, parishes as such developed much more slowly. It still remained possible for the bishop personally to minister to the faithful. Another solution was found to cope with the increase of new Christians. Other centers of worship known as cemeterial, filial or title *(titulares)* churches were established wherein liturgical functions could be performed. These, however, were not the equivalent of parish churches, but remained for centuries what in their erection they were intended to be, that is to say, merely supplementary churches. So much so was this true that the obligation of Sunday Mass had still to be fulfilled at the bishop's cathedral. Accordingly, with the possible exception of Rome and Alexandria, parishes did not come into existence in the cities until the eleventh century.

From the eleventh century, therefore, parishes began to spring up in the cities. But the introduction of the new discipline did not take place in all cities at the same time. Some cities were at that time divided into parishes; others did not see the change until much later. Indeed, even at the time of the Council of Trent cities could still be found wherein the parochial discipline had not yet been introduced. This is evidenced by the fact that in 1563 the Fathers of the Council decreed that all bishops in those *cities* and places where there were as yet no parish churches should see to their erection as quickly as possible.[12]

Finally, the Congregation of the Propagation of the Faith ordered for those regions subjected to its jurisdiction that in missions lands, in accord with the mind of the Council of Trent, parishes be established as quickly as possible.[13]

Article 3. The Concept of Parishes According to the Code

Canon 216, § 1. Territorium cuiuslibet dioecesis dividatur in distinctas partes territoriales; unicuique autem parti sua peculiaris ecclesia cum populo determinato est assignanda, suusque peculiaris rector, tanquam proprius eiusdem pastor, est praeficiendus pro necessaria animarum cura.

§ 2. Pari modo vicariatus apostolicus et praefectura apostolica, ubi commode fieri possit, dividatur.

§ 3. Partes dioecesis de quibus in § 1, sunt *paroeciae;* partes vicariatus apostolici ac praefecturae apostolicae, si peculiaris rector eiusdem fuerit assignatus, appellantur *quasi-paroeciae.*

§ 4. Non possunt sine speciali apostolico indulto constitui paroeciae pro diversitate sermonis seu nationis fidelium in eadem civitate vel territorio degentium, nec paroeciae mere familiares aut personales; ad constitutas autem quod attinet, nihil innovandum, inconsulta Apostolica Sede

Canon 216, § 1, embodies the command that the territory of every diocese shall be divided into distinct territorial sections, and each portion shall have its own proper church to which the Catholic population of the district shall be assigned. Such a

[12] Conc. Trident., sess. XXIV, *de ref.*, c. 13.

[13] S. C. de Prop. Fide, litt. encycl. (ad Deleg. Ap. pro Oriente), 8 nov. 1882 — *Collectanea S. Congregationis de Propaganda Fide* (2 vols., Romae, 1907), n. 1578; S. C. de Prop. Fide, litt. encycl. (ad Ep. Indiar.), 28 aug. 1893 — *Collectanea*, n. 1848.

church is to be presided over by a rector, as the proper pastor for the necessary care of souls.

This canon, it is true, uses only the word *diocese;* but what is stated here concerning dioceses must be understood as applying in like manner to abbeys and prelatures *nullius,* for, in law, the term *diocese* refers also to abbeys or prelatures *nullius* unless the nature of things or the context show the contrary.[14] Canon 216, § 1, however, contains no exception for abbeys or prelatures *nullius;* hence the conclusion stands that they too must be included under the provision of this canon.

The Council of Trent, long before the Code, had already ordered that every diocese be divided into parishes just as quickly as possible.[15] The words of the Code in canon 216, § 1, however, are much stronger in that they do not command that dioceses be divided into parishes "as quickly as possible" *(quamprimum),* but rather, without any qualification, decree absolutely *(dividatur)* that parishes be established.

Canon 216, § 1, concerns itself only with *dioceses* or the territories within the Church subject to the common law, under the direct and immediate supervision of the Sacred Consistorial Congregation.[16] Accordingly, for mission lands or for those localities which are subject to the Sacred Congregation of the Propagation of the Faith, an analogous division of territory is ordered in canon 216, § 2, which states that the vicariates and prefectures apostolic shall be divided in like manner, where it can conveniently be done.

What is stated here in the Code had already been ordered upon different occasions by the Sacred Congregation of the Propagation of the Faith.[17] Subsequently, the same Sacred Congregation explained that the division should be made even

14 Canon 215, § 2.

15 ". . . In iis civitatibus, ac locis, ubi nullae sunt parochiales, *quamprimum* fieri curent (episcopi)." — Conc. Trident., sess. XXIV, *de ref.,* c. 13.

16 Canon 248, § 2.

17 S. C. de Prop. Fide, litt. encyl. (ad Deleg. Ap. pro Oriente), 8 nov., 1882 — *Collectanea,* n. 1578; S. C. de Prop. Fide, litt. encyl. (ad Ep. Indiar.), 28 aug. 1893 — *Collectanea,* n. 1848.

in those parts of the prefectures or vicariates where it could be usefully accomplished, without the necessity of awaiting a time when the whole prefecture or vicariate could be likewise divided.[18]

Here again in canon 216, §§ 1, 2, a difference in the wording can be detected. The legislator, when treating of dioceses, seems to recognize no reason which would render impossible or impracticable the division of a diocese into separate sections; accordingly, the provision of the canon is absolute.[19] On the other hand, the Code seems to be aware of the fact that frequently a similar division of a prefecture or vicariate would be impossible, difficult, or, at least, impracticable; wherefore, the provision of canon 216, § 2, is conditional in that it orders the division wherever it can be conveniently accomplished.[20] The sections into which a diocese has been divided are called by the Code *parishes;* the corresponding portions of a prefecture or vicariate apostolic are called *quasi-parishes.*[21]

It can hardly be stated, however, that canon 216 offers a generic definition of a parish. At most, it gives a description thereof. Indeed, nowhere in the Code can a *generic* definition of a parish be found. True, canon 216 is quite clear in what it does offer, but the point is that a generic definition of a parish seems to be lacking therein.

The usual procedure is first to define an object generically, and only then to proceed to a consideration of the various species into which it is divided. In Book III, by way of example, the Code first gives a definition of a benefice in general;[22] and only after having done so does it proceed to a consideration of the various kinds of benefices.[23] In the case of parishes, however, the Code in canon 216, § 1, proceeds immediately to a description of a *territorial* parish, without having first defined a parish as

18 S. C. de Prop. Fide, instr., 24 iul., 1920 — *Acta Apostolicae Sedis, Commentarium Officiale* (Romae, 1909—), XII (1920), 331.

19 Canon 216, § 1. *Dividatur* territorium cuiuslibet diocesis . . .

20 Canon 216, § 2. ". . . *ubi commode fieri possit,* dividantur."

21 Canon 216, § 3.

22 Canon 1409.

23 Canon 1411.

such. In other words, a species of parish is described therein; not the genus as such. Hence, it is legitimate to conclude that neither here nor elsewhere in the Code is the generic definition of a parish as such to be found.

What, then, is the generic definition of a parish, and what are its constituent elements?

Maroto defines a parish in general as any distinct and lesser part into which a diocese or quasi-diocese has been divided for the express purpose of exercising the particular and immediate care of souls, consisting of a particularly designated church and a determined group of people under the supervision of a particular rector who is called its pastor.[24]

The constituent elements or proper characteristics of a parish in general according to Maroto are, therefore, three:[25]

1. A parish must constitute a *distinct part* of a diocese, whether the partition be made by reason of *territorial circumscription*, or whether it have as its basis the *personal characteristics* of the people who dwell therein, such as, language, nationality, or diversity of rite.

Many authors in discussing this point enumerate a distinct *territory* as a constituent part of a parish.[26] Although this is very often, indeed, in the majority of cases, true, yet it would seem incorrect to require a distinct *territory* in the generic definition of a parish. For a so-called "national" parish is just as much a parish in every sense of the word as is a territorial parish. Yet it may exist without any definite territorial circumscription

24 "Paroecia ad sensum novi Codicis est in genere unaquaeque ex distinctis partibus in quas dioecesis aliqua vel quasi-dioecesis ad peculiarem et immediatam animarum curam gerendam cum sua peculiari ecclesia assignata, determinato populo adscripto, suoque peculiari rectore, tamquam proprio eiusdem pastore, praefecto, qui sane peculiaris rector dicitur parochus." — *Institutiones Iuris Canonici* ,II, n. 771.

25 *Institutiones Iuris Canonici, loc. cit.*

26 Augustine (+ 1943), *The Canonical and Civil Status of Catholic Parishes in the United States* (St. Louis: B. Herder Book Co., 1926), p. 2; Fanfani, *De Iure Parochorum ad Normam Codicis Iuris Canonici* (Romae: Marietti, 1924), pp. 2-3; Cocchi, *Commentarium in Codicem Iuris Canonici* (5 vols., 3. ed., Taurinorum Augustae: Marietti, 1931-1938), II (1932), n. 145; Connolly, *The Canonical Erection of Parishes*, p. 3.

whatsoever. Thus, for instance, in an exceedingly small diocese it could happen that all the persons of a certain nationality, language, or rite within that diocese would pertain to a particular national parish. Here there would be no parochial circumscription other than that of the diocese itself. Their limits would be identical. Notwithstanding this, the fact that these persons constitute a particular *part* or section of the diocese, not a particular *territory,* is sufficient to classify their parish as a true canonical parish in every sense of the word, all the other requisites, of course, being present.

2. This division of a diocese into separate parts must have as its special purpose *(ratio formalis)* the facilitating or fostering of the particular care of souls.

3. This particular section of the diocese must have the following material elements:

a. Every parish must have a church proper unto itself. It is not essential that the church be actually constructed at the time the parish is founded. There must, however, be present the intention of erecting a church, especially designated for this group of people. Some other edifice may be used in the meantime.

b. Every parish must have its own proper pastor. Again it is not essential that there be physically present at all times the person of the pastor himself. Accordingly, a parish does not cease to be a parish merely because its pastor has been transferred to another parish, or has, perhaps, died, and no other has as yet been appointed in his stead. It would be better, therefore, to state that it is the office of pastor rather than the person of the pastor himself which must be permanently established in every canonical parish.

c. Finally, every parish must have a determined group of people pertaining thereto. As already mentioned above, this determination may be made either by reason of the territory in which these people live, or by reason of their personal characteristics, such as language, nationality, or rite. In the former case, the inhabitants of this particular parish become parishioners by acquiring a domicile or quasi-domicile within the limits of the parish itself.[27]

In the latter case, the members of a national parish become parishioners thereof by the fact that they are of a certain nationality, speak a particular language, or practice a special rite, with the added fact that some parish has been designated to meet their particular needs. So much, however, are national parishes the exception to the general rules of ecclesiastical discipline that the Code prescribes that parishes are not to be erected for the faithful of a different nationality or of a different language without an apostolic indult; national parishes already established are not to be changed without consultation with the Holy See.[28]

In closing this article, one must give some consideration to the various kinds of parishes as they appear in the Code of Canon Law. This is deemed necessary, since references to these specific types of parishes will appear later in this work.

Parishes are, therefore, divided as follows into:

a. Parishes *(stricte dictae)* and quasi-parishes *(late dictae)*. The former are the resultant parts of the division of a diocese; the latter are the canonical partitions of a prefecture or vicariate apostolic.

Too much emphasis must not, however, be placed upon this division so as to imply that quasi-parishes share only by similarity or participation with parishes properly so called. For quasi-parishes, if really such, are canonical parishes in every sense of the word; and the Code itself considers them as of equal rank when it states that quasi-pastors are, with all parochial rights and obligations, equal to pastors, and come in law under the name of pastors.[29] There are, however, some exceptions to this general rule.[30]

So much are parishes and quasi-parishes of the same legal nature that Maroto maintains, and in the opinion of the writer

27 Canon 94, § 1. Sive per domicilium sive per quasi-domicilium suum quisque parochum et Ordinarium sortitur.

28 Canon 216, § 4.

29 Canon 451, § 2, 1°.

30 Canon 454, § 4; 457; 466, § 1.

with justification, that if, perchance, an Apostolic prefecture or vicariate were to become a diocese, its quasi-parishes would *ipso facto* become parishes, without the necessity of an intervening decree of erection. So, too, on the other hand, if a part of a diocese should be dismembered and made into a prefecture or vicariate, the parishes of that dismembered section would automatically become quasi-parishes. And the reason in both cases would be fundamentally the same. For the distinction between a parish and a quasi-parish is to be sought, not in the juridical nature of the institutes themselves, but in the relationship which they may or may not, as the case may be, bear to an established hierarchy of organization.

b. *Territorial* and *non-territorial.* This distinction has already been sufficiently discussed.

c. *Secular* and *religious.* A secular parish is a parish whose *title* pertains to the secular clergy. A religious parish, on the other hand, is to be conferred in *title* upon a religious community.[31]

d. *Independent* and *incorporated.* An independent parish is one which exists by itself apart from any consideration of another moral person with which it might have been united. An incorporated parish, on the other hand, is one which has been united, by proper authority, with some other moral person.[32]

e. *Movable* and *immovable.* This final division is founded upon the degree of stability enjoyed by the pastor in the exercise of his office.[33]

Article 4. The Modification of Parishes

In this final article of the Preliminary Notions it has seemed opportune to furnish some general notions concerning the possible modifications of a parish. Practically all authors treat of this subject under the title of the *innovation* of benefices.[34]

31 This distinction will be discussed later in greater detail. *Cf. infra*, p. 83.

32 *Infra*, pp. 72-74.

33 Canons 454, §§ 1-3; 2147-2156; 2157-2161.

34 Wernz, *Ius Decretalium*, II, n. 254; Pistocchi, *De Re Beneficiali*

The choice of the word "innovation" is a happy one for those who have written of this matter in Latin. In English, however, although the word "innovation" does actually signify any change in an established order, still the use of the word itself is rather inadequate in the present case. Wherefore, to avoid confusion and in order to give in a single word the precise idea of the matter to be treated in this article, the writer has chosen the term "modification" in preference to the usual word "innovation".

Before proceeding to a consideration of the modifications which may be encountered in a parish, however, one may well trace briefly the possible span of life, if such it can be called, of a parish as a moral person.

The existence and vicissitudes of a parish can be divided into four phases. These four phases are not actually to be found in every canonical parish; they are, however, *possible* in every parish. The first phase is concerned with the very coming into existence or the erection of the parish. The second phase is related to the parish, already established, as continuing its existence under normal conditions. In the third phase any or all changes in the parish which alter its original status are to be considered. These changes may concern either the rights, the obligations, the location, or the species of the parish. Lastly, in the fourth and final phase consideration can be given to the passing out of existence or the suppression of the life of this moral person known as a parish. The Code of Canon Law contains explicit legislation concerning each of these phases, whether actual or possible, in the span of life of a parish in the light of its moral personality.

Section 1. The First Phase in the Life of a Parish

With regard to the first phase, legislation for the canonical erection of parishes concerning the necessary competence of the

(Taurini: Marietti, 1928), p. 65; Coronata, *Institutiones Iuris Canonici* (5 vols., Taurini: Marietti, 1928-1936), II, nn. 979-986; d'Angelo (1885-1930), "Il Diritto Canonico," — *Il Monitore Ecclesiastico* (Roma, 1876 —), XXXII (1920), 291-293.

superior, for the material requirements, for the respecting of the rights of third parties, and regarding conditions established in the act of foundation is to be found under the general legislation for the erection of benefices.[35]

Some authors hold that a parish can be erected according to two possible methods. Indeed, Connolly states that "there are actually only two modes of erecting new parishes, namely, by creation and by division."[36]

If by "creation," in a wide sense, one were to understand the bringing into existence of a parish which up until the present has not been in existence, either because there had never been a parish in this locality at any time, or because an extinctive union has furnished the basis for the erection of this new parish, or, finally, because a parish which had once been suppressed is now restored to its former status, then of a certainty it would seem correct to limit the possible modes for the erection of parishes to two, namely, by way of division, and by way of creation.

But if, one the other hand, one were to restrict the sense of the word "creation" and understand thereby only the formation of a new moral person out of *new* territory — and this seems to be the understanding of the term as used by Connolly[37] — then the writer feels that the division which would limit the modes for the erection of parishes to but two, namely, by way of creation and by way of division, is not adequate.

The Code in canon 1419 describes an extinctive union as one in which out of two or more suppressed benefices a single new benefice is brought into being. Suppose, therefore, that circumstances have rendered impossible, or at least impracticable, the continuance of two parishes. With the necessary permission of the Holy See an extinctive union is decided upon and actually effected. As a result of this union a new parish is erected. Can not, therefore, an extinctive union be considered as a method for the erection of a parish? And yet this is brought about neither

35 Canons 1414-1418; Connolly, *The Canonical Erection of Parishes*, pp. 47-95.

36 *The Canonical Erection of Parishes*, p. 44.

37 *Op. cit.*, pp. 45-46.

by way of creation out of new territory, as the term "creation" is referred to by Connolly, nor by way of division.

Moreover, circumstances may dictate the necessity of re-establishing a parish which, upon being in existence for a time, was eventually suppressed. A transaction such as this is, in effect, tantamount to the erection of a new parish; but in no way can it be contended that the erection of this new parish takes place from new territory, nor by way of division of an already existing parish. Wherefore, it seems more acceptable to the writer to state that there are actually four methods that can be followed in the erection of a new parish.

A parish can be erected by way of creation out of new territory, that is to say, out of a territory that up until now has never had a parish of any kind within its confines. Secondly, and this is the point which is of particular interest in this work, a parish may be created as the result of an extinctive union effected between two other parishes whereby the latter cease to exist and the former comes into existence. Thirdly, a new parish may be created by the restoration of an already suppressed parish to its former status. Lastly, a parish may be erected by dividing an already existing parish into two or more new parishes. These four methods, so it seems to the writer, exhaust the possibilities to be encountered in the erection of a parish.

Section 2. The Second Possible Phase in the Life of a Parish

The second possible phase in the life of a parish as a moral person considers the parish as continuing in its existence in that state in which it was first erected. Nothing has occurred to disturb that original status. If such be the case, and it usually is, at least for a time, legislation to regulate such a parish in its peaceful existence is likewise to be found in the Code.[38]

Section 3. The Third Phase Possible in the Life of a Parish

The third phase possible in the life of a parish as a moral person is the one which constitutes the matter for particular consideration in this article. It has already been stated that this

38 Canons 1431-1447; 1472-1483; 1497-1517; 1518-1528; 1529-1543.

third phase considers any and all alterations or modifications in the original status of the parish.

A modification of a parish is any change in its original status which affects the rights, spiritual or temporal, the obligations, the location, or the species of the parish.[39] So long as any one of these elements has been altered, the parish must be said to have undergone a modification.

It is of the utmost importance to stress the idea that the modification of a parish does not imply the cessation of the parish. That is to say, a modification, radical though it may be, must leave in existence at least some part of the original parish. Thus, in an extinctive union, though the parishes involved may entirely lose their moral personality, yet at least the rights and obligations which were theirs continue to exist in the new parish resulting from the union. And if these rights conflict, at least the more favorable ones continue in existence.

In a mutually co-ordinative union the parishes themselves objectively remain as they were; the modification affects only the pastors. In a collaterally subordinative union, on the contrary, one parish is subjected to the other; but both remain as moral persons. So, too, in the division of a parish, though a part may be taken to form a new parish, at least some part of the original parish remains as a parish. Should the modification of a parish consist of its change of site, the parish as a moral person or benefice remains intact; only its location is changed. Finally, should the modification consist of the dismemberment of its territory or property, by proper authority, at least a part of the original parish remains in existence.

A modification of a parish, therefore, is a change in the parish which is effected without destroying the parish in its entirety. Should the modification be urged to such an extent that the parish in its entirety ceases to exist, then one is confronted with not the modification, but the suppression of a parish. Where-

[39] Wernz, *Ius Decretalium,* II, n. 254; Laurentius (1861-1927), *Institutiones Iuris Ecclesiastici* (Friburgi Brisgoviae, 1903), n. 236; Prümmer (1866-1931), *Manuale Iuris Ecclesiastici* (ed. altera, 2 vols., Friburgi Brisgoviae, 1920), II, 363.

fore, though the Code treats of the suppression of benefices along with their union, division, change of site, dismemberment, and transmutation,[40] strictly considered, suppression cannot be classified among the *modifications* of benefices, or, as the older canonists called them, their *innovations*.[41]

Any modification of a parish whatsoever must be considered in law as a matter of onerous and *odious* character. Those responsible for the foundation of a parish can be considered as having entered into a tacit contract whereby they received the assurance that the rights and obligations decided upon in the act of foundation will be observed and discharged.[42] Any form of modification in the parish, however, is a deviation from this assurance. Wherefore, even though there be no particular founders whose rights are to be respected, yet in those benefices which are well established, any form of modification is fundamentally to be discouraged.[43] This does not mean that modifications in a parish are not under any circumstances whatsoever permissible; on the contrary, they are permissible, and indeed, a matter of necessity and not of mere option, when the requirements envisaged by the law are actually present. It does mean, however, in view of the fact that modifications are by their very nature odious, that the scope of the law which makes them allowable must be subjected to strict interpretation.[44]

The Code, besides its particular legislation concerning the various forms of the modification of benefices,[45] contains general norms to be followed by all in any kind of modification whatsoever.[46]

In any kind of modification of parishes the intervention of a competent superior is required. For some types the Holy See alone is competent; for other types, provided that the restric-

40 Canons 1419-1430.

41 "Ad innovationem non pertinet suppressio quae est beneficii cessatio." — Coronata, *Institutiones Iuris Canonici,* II, n. 979.

42 Laurentius, *Institutiones Iuris Canonici,* n. 236.

43 Conc. Trident., sess. XXIV, *de ref.,* c. 5.

44 Canon 19.

45 Canons 1422-1425; 1426; 1427; 1430.

46 Canons 1428, §§ 1, 2, 3.

tions stipulated in the law are observed, the local Ordinary is also competent.[47] Secondly, in order that proof of the modification of a benefice be obtainable in the external forum, a document explaining the nature of the modification should be drawn up at the time the modification is effected. A more detailed explanation of this document and a discussion of the sanction imposed when it is absent will be furnished later. As a third general requirement for any form of the modification of a parish it is necessary that the advice of the Cathedral Chapter or of the diocesan consultors, as the case may warrant, be obtained. The question of the validity of any modification effected without the due observance of this prescription of law will likewise be discussed more in detail in a subsequent part of this work.[48]

A fourth general requirement in any form of modification concerns the necessity of a just cause for the validity of the modification itself. The nature of the cause may differ according to the type of modification which has been effected in the parish. The necessity of some just cause is, however, a factor common to all forms of modification. Finally, recourse against any act of modification in a parish by the local Ordinary is granted, but only *in devolutivo*. A more complete discussion of this recourse with reference to the union of parishes will also be given later in this work.[49]

The *particular* forms of the modification of benefices as enumerated in the Code are the following: the union, transference of site, division, dismemberment, and transmutation of benefices. A brief notion of each will suffice here since they do not constitute the subject matter of this work. As to the notion of the union of benefices and its juridical effects, because of the complications in this matter, and since it constitutes the precise matter of this dissertation, it has been deemed advisable to treat of this subject at greater length in a later chapter.

The *transference of site* of a parish is realized when the seat of the benefice is changed from one place to another. The *divi-*

47 Canons 1423-1424; 1426; 1427; 1430.

48 *Infra*, p. 141.

49 *Infra*, p. 133.

sion of a parish occurs when two or more parishes are formed out of what was formerly a single parish. *Dismemberment* occurs when a part of the territory of a parish or part of its goods is withdrawn and assigned to some other benefice, or to a charitable cause, or to some other ecclesiastical institution. *Transmutation* of a parish signifies a change in the species of the parish itself. Thus, should a secular parish by competent authority be changed into a religious parish, in the strict sense of the term, such a parish can be said to have undergone a transmutation in the canonical sense of the word.[50]

Section 4. The Fourth and Final Phase in the Life of a Parish

The fourth and final phase in the life of a parish as a moral person is realized when it is found necessary to terminate the very existence of the parish by means of its total suppression. As has already been pointed out, however, since nothing whatever remains of the parish after its suppression, suppression cannot be rightly enumerated among the modes of *modification*, for modification requires that at least some vestige of the parish so affected remain even after the act of modification has been fully executed.

50 Canon 1421.

CHAPTER II

PARISHES ARE ECCLESIASTICAL BENEFICES

The rôle which the present chapter is to have in this entire work is, indeed, of the greatest importance. The Code in canons 1419-1430 treats of the possible change in status, not of parishes in particular, but of benefices in general. Legislation concerning the union of parishes, it is true, is to be found in these canons; but there are also to be found therein canons which treat of the union of *benefices* in general, which canons must also be considered if the commentary is to be complete. Hence, one can readily understand why it is important to establish from the very outset the fact that parishes are ecclesiastical benefices. Moreover, the present chapter reflects an added importance when one recalls the doubts which existed over a period of time as to the legal nature of many of our American parishes. If the norms concerning the union of benefices are to be applied to our American parishes, then it must first be established that these parishes are, in reality, true benefices.

For a full realization of the purpose set forth in this chapter, it will first be necessary to give some notions of the origin of a benefice, and, in particular, of its essential elements. These elements will then be related to that canonical institute known as the parish, and if it is found that all the elements of a benefice are present, then the conclusion must of necessity follow that a parish is a benefice.

Article 1. The Nature and Elements of a Benefice

The word *beneficium* in antiquity was first used to signify that portion of land or of the manor given by the Emperor to his soldiers, in recognition of faithful service, as a means of their support. *Ecclesiastical* benefices, however, are derived from the ancient system of administering church property. In the early days of the Church all ecclesiastical goods formed one common fund and were administered by the bishop. These goods were divided into four parts (three in Spain), one of which was designated for the support of the clergy.[1]

As time went on, changes were introduced into this unity of the administration of church property. This change was effected particularly in consequence of offerings and foundations which were attributed to particular churches. As early as the fifth century, especially in the rural districts, the bishop had begun, at the request of his priests *(precaria)*, to grant the use of these foundations or offerings in real estate as a means of support for the individual priest in charge of particular churches. These concessions continued to grow until they became the universal practice, so that by the sixth century the administration and use of this property became so proper a function for the priest in charge of the church to which it had been conceded that no longer could the bishop arbitrarily deprive him of its income. Finally, the dominion as well as the administration of this property was recognized as proper to the church to which it had been granted, so that whosoever governed the church obtained the right to sustenance from the income of the property attached thereto. In this right to the income of the property, a right founded in the parochial office with which an individual priest was vested, is to be found the beginning of parochial benefices.[2] From the viewpoint of history, therefore, it can be stated that the early rural parishes became benefices almost as soon as they became parishes.[3]

An ecclesiastical benefice is defined by the Code as a juridical entity established or erected in perpetuity by competent ecclesiastical authority, and consisting of a sacred office with which is associated the right to receive the revenue from the endowment

1 Cf. the letters of Popes Simplicius (468-483) and Gelasius I (492-496) — Thiel, *Epistolae Romanorum Pontificum a S. Hilario usque ad S. Hormisdam* (Brunsbergae, 1868), pp. 175, 178, 381; cf. also, cc. 26-31, C. XII, q. 2.

2 Cf. c. 61, C. XVI, q. 1.

3 *Supra*, pp. 4-6.

annexed to the office.[4] The definition as proffered by the Code is quite clear in itself. Yet, for the purpose indicated at the beginning of this chapter, it will be necessary to apportion the definition into its various parts in order to gain a thorough understanding of each. It is, therefore, stated that a benefice is:

a. *A Juridical Entity.* The Code by using the words *"juridical entity"* classifies a benefice as a non-collegiate moral person, that is to say, as the subject which sustains the rights and obligations inherent in the benefice itself, for the subject of all rights and obligations must be a person, whether physical or moral. There can be no doubt that a benefice is a non-collegiate moral person, for the Code itself expressly states that in the Church, besides physical persons, there are also moral persons established by public authority, which are divided into collegiate moral persons and non-collegiate moral persons, such as churches, Seminaries, benefices, etc.[5]

A benefice is, therefore, first and foremost, a moral person, consisting of two elements, viz.: a sacred office, and the right to the revenue from the endowment connected with such an office. The property of perpetuity must be considered as pertaining in a special manner not to either of the two constituent elements in question, but rather to the juridical entity or moral person itself. To this same moral person must be attributed the ownership or dominion over the endowment, with all the rights consequent thereto, such as those of acquiring property, of contracting obligations, and of vindicating its rights. Since in law, however, all moral persons are considered as minors,[6] they must be represented by a major physical person.[7] This function is performed by the beneficiary or incumbent of the benefice, who is consid-

[4] Canon 1409. Beneficium ecclesiasticum est ens juridicum a competente ecclesiastica auctoritate in perpetuum constitutum seu erectum, constans officio sacro et iure percipiendi reditus ex dote officio adnexos.

[5] Canon 99. In Ecclesia, praeter personas physicas, sunt etiam personae morales, publica auctoritate constitutae, quae distinguuntur in personas morales collegiales et non collegiales, ut ecclesiae, Seminaria, beneficia, etc.

[6] Canon 100, § 3. Personae morales sive collegiales sive non collegiales minoribus aequiparantur.

[7] Cf. canon 1648, §§ 1-3.

ered before the law as the representative of the moral person, its administrator, or its usufructuary.[8]

b. *Establishment or Erection of a Benefice.* Canon 1409 indicates the manner in which the juridic personality of a benefice is acquired. The Catholic Church and the Apostolic See have the nature of a moral person by Divine ordinance. All other inferior moral persons acquire their personality either from the law itself, or by a special concession of the competent ecclesiastical superior given by means of a formal decree for the purpose of religion or charity.[9] Hence, in the erection of a benefice it is not sufficient that the *mere approbation* of the competent superior be obtained for the joining of the right to the fruits of the endowment with some particular office. Such approbation would not be sufficient to establish the benefice as a moral person. In order to accomplish this, there must be an act of *positive intervention* on the part of a competent ecclesiastical superior by means of a formal decree in which it is positively stated that for the future a determined right to the revenues of some particular endowment is thereby joined to some particular office. Then and only then does the benefice become a legally recognized moral person.

c. *Perpetuity of a Benefice.* Two kinds of perpetuity are possible in a benefice, *objective* perpetuity and *subjective* perpetuity. The former is founded on the condition of the benefice itself, the latter on the condition of the beneficiary. If the benefice has been founded so that of itself it will not cease to be but will only be vacated, then objective perpetuity is said to be present. If, on the other hand, the benefice has been conferred for the lifetime of its incumbent, in addition it also possesses what is known as subjective perpetuity.

It has been stated that both types of perpetuity are *possible* in a benefice. The question now arises as to whether both types are *essential.* In other words, must a benefice to be a true benefice possess both objective and subjective perpetuity?

8 D'Angelo, "Il Codice di Diritto Canonico," — *Il Monitore Ecclesiastico* (Roma, 1876 —), XXXII (1920), 288-290.

9 Canon 100, § 1.

Up until the time of the Code, authors were not in accord in defining a benefice. Particular difficulty was experienced in ascertaining whether the property of perpetuity was to be assigned to the sacred office, that is, to the spiritual element, or rather to the right to the revenue from the income of the endowment, that is, to the temporal element. Authors are now, and always have been, in accord in requiring that a benfice possess at least objective perpetuity.[10] The same unanimity, however, is not to be found among pre-Code authors with regard to the necessity of subjective perpetuity. Not a few authors insisted that subjective perpetuity was so essential to the nature of a true benefice that without it no benefice could be had.[11]

This disagreement among the authors is nothing other than the counterpart to the controversy as to the definition of a benefice. As has already been pointed out, authors before the Code continued to disagree among themselves as to which element in a benefice should be given primary consideration, the sacred office, or the right to the income of the endowment. Theologians were inclined to stress the spiritual element or sacred office to such an extent that they defined a benefice as the right to the exercise of a sacred office constituted by ecclesiastical authority to which the right to the income of the endowment was attached. The sacred office was for them, then, the primary consideration; the right to the income was merely accessory.[12]

Canonists, on the other hand, insisting upon the historical development of benefices, and adverting to the fact that sacred

10 Schmalzgrueber (1663-1735), *Jus Ecclesiasticum Universum* (5 vols. in 12, Romae, 1843-1845), lib. III, tit. V, n. 4; Reiffenstuel (1641-1703), *Jus Canonicum Universum* (6 vols., Romae, 1831-1834), lib. III, tit. V, nn. 6, 8, 17; Garcia (+ after 1613), *De Beneficiis Ecclesiasticis Amplissimus et Doctissimus Tractatus* (Venetiis, 1618), pars I, cap. 2, n. 79; Cocchi, *Commentarium in Codicem Iuris Canonici,* III, n. 81; Wernz-Vidal, *Ius Canonicum ad Codicis normam exactum* (7 vols. in 8, Romae: Aedes Universitatis Gregorianae, 1923-1938), II² (1928), n. 141, nota 3; Pistocchi, *De Re Beneficiali iuxta Canones,* p. 9.

11 Cf. Reiffenstuel, lib. III, tit. V, n. 8; for the contrary opinion, cf.: Garcia, *De Beneficiis,* pars I, cap. II, nn. 2, 65.

12 Suarez (1548-1617), *Opera Omnia* (ed. nova, 26 vols. and 2 Indices, Parisiis, 1856-1866), XIII, 760, nn. 1, 2.

offices had existed for some time independently of benefices, chose to stress the temporal element as that which specifically constituted a benefice. Wherefore, they defined a benefice as the perpetual right to the income from church property coming to a cleric by reason of a spiritual office, a right constituted by ecclesiastical authority.[13] From the definition of a benefice rendered by these canonists as the perpetual right to the income of church property *(ius perpetuum percipiendi fructus)* it can readily be seen why they required subjective perpetuity in a benefice.

The Code of Canon Law, however, has solved the question on an entirely different basis by linking the definition of a benefice with the theory of moral persons. Accordingly, the type of perpetuity required in a benefice is no longer to be ascertained from a consideration of the elements which compose the benefice, that is to say, of the sacred office, or of the right to the revenue from the endowment, but rather from a consideration of the nature of a benefice as a moral person *(ens juridicum)*.

The Code in canon 102 states that a moral person is by its very nature perpetual. The perpetuity expressed in this canon is objective perpetuity. Therefore, since a moral person is by its very nature perpetual, and since a benefice is a moral person, every benefice must have at least objective perpetuity.

It can no longer be stated, however, that subjective perpetuity is an essential note of a benefice: The Code in canon 1411, 4°, distinguishes between manual benefices and perpetual benefices. The former are conferred in a revocable manner; the latter are conferred in perpetuity. Since the Code defines a manual benefice as one which is conferred in a revocable manner, and yet classifies it as a true benefice, it must follow that subjective perpetuity cannot be of the essence of a benefice.

d. *The Ecclesiastical Authority Competent To Erect a Benefice.* This condition required in the erection of a benefice follows from its constituent elements, for a benefice arises from the union of a sacred office with the right to the revenue from the endow-

13 Reiffenstuel, *loc. cit.*, n. 6.; Schmalzgrueber, *loc. cit.*, n. 2.

ment. The Church alone, however, is competent in the erection of spiritual offices.[14] The civil authority as well as a private person can supply the endowment for the office, but the actual union of the endowment with the sacred office depends entirely upon ecclesiastical authority.[15]

A moral person receives its personality from the perfect homogeneous juridic person to which it is subjected. Accordingly, with regard to the erection of benefices in the light of their moral personality, the competent juridic person will be either the supreme ecclesiastical authority, the Holy See, or some other person, whether physical or moral, to whom this power has been expressly committed by the supreme authority.[16] The persons competent in the erection of benefices are determined in canon 1414, §§ 1-4.

e. *The Benefice Consists of a Sacred Office.* Canon 1409 indicates one of the two essential elements of any benefice. The sacred element is the principal element, and, as it were, the cause and foundation of the second or temporal element according to the rule of Boniface VIII (1294-1303) whereby a benefice is conferred because of a sacred office.[17]

According to the provision of canon 145, § 2, the term *office* must be taken in the strict sense of the word since in canon 1409 the contrary is not apparent from the context.[18] An office in the strict sense of the term is a permanent function or charge created either by divine or ecclesiastical law, conferred according to the rules of the sacred canons, and entailing at least some participation in ecclesiastical power, whether of orders or of jurisdiction.[19]

14 De Meester, *Juris Canonici et Juris Canonico-Civilis Compendium* (ed. nova, 3 vols. in 4, Brugis: Desclée, 1921-1928), III (1926), n. 1393.

15 Vermeersch-Creusen, *Epitome Iuris Canonici* (3 vols., Romae: Dessain, Vol. I, 6. ed., 1937; Vol. II, 5. ed., 1934; Vol. III, 5. ed., 1936), II, n. 742.

16 Coronata, *Institutiones Iuris Canonici*, II, n. 972.

17 C. 15, *de rescriptis*, I, 3, in VI°.

18 Canon 145, § 2. In iure officium ecclesiasticum accipitur stricto sensu, nisi aliud ex contextu appareat.

19 Canon 145, § 1; Woywod (1880-1941), *A Practical Commentary on the Code of Canon Law* (6th printing, 2 vols., New York: Joseph F. Wagner, 1941), I, 60.

This office, whether or not forming part of a benefice, cannot be validly conferred without the canonical appointment thereto, that is to say, unless the concession of the office be made by a competent ecclesiastical authority in accordance with the norms enacted in the canons.[20]

Finally, insomuch as an office in its strict sense implies a partial exercise of the power of orders or of ecclesiastical jurisdiction, it follows that an office in its strict sense cannot be conferred upon anyone who is not a cleric.[21]

f. *The Right to Revenue Contained in a Benefice.* This right to the revenue constitutes the second element of any benefice. By means of this right a benefice is formally constituted in the realm of benefices, and is specifically distinguished from all other sacred offices which are, because of its absence, devoid of the nature of benefices. It is to be noted that canon 1409 requires only the right to the revenues *(et iure percipiendi reditus)*; it does not require the actual receipt thereof. Should, therefore, a beneficiary who is sufficiently provided for with this world's goods from other sources decline to accept the revenues of his benefice, the benefice does not for this reason cease to be a benefice. The actual receipt of the revenue is not essential to the nature of a benefice; it is sufficient that the right to this revenue be conferred. It is not necessary that the right itself be exercised.[22] Wherefore, as shall be seen presently, it is not even necessary that the property whence the revenue is derived be in the actual possession of the beneficiary, so long as the right to the revenue is his. Although, therefore, some form of property *(bona)* is required in constituting a benefice, it is not the property itself but the right to the revenue from it which formally constitutes the element essential for a benefice.[23]

g. *The Endowment of a Benefice.* The endowment constitutes the purely temporal element of a benefice according to the distinction made by canonists whereby three elements can be

20 Canon 147, §§ 1, 2.

21 Canon 118.

22 Cf. Canon 1473.

23 Pistocchi, *De Re Beneficiali*, p. 13.

distinguished in a benefice: the spiritual element, the temporal annexed to the spiritual, and the purely temporal.[24] The spiritual element is the sacred office itself. The temporal annexed to the spiritual is the right to the revenue from the endowment. The purely temporal element is the endowment itself.

In the matter of the endowment *(dos)*, more than in any other single point on its legislation on benefices, the Code has introduced radical changes. Originally, in Catholic countries, the endowment for a benefice was established by setting aside a quantity of property *(bona)* sufficient to sustain the beneficiary from its income. It was required that this property be in real estate, or that it be immovable goods, or, at least, that the endowment be invested in immovable goods. Moreover, this property had to come under the direct dominion of the Church, which did not erect the benefice until it had been received as such. With its acceptance by the Church it became ecclesiastical property *(bona ecclesiastica)*, subject to the special laws of the Church concerning alienation and administration. This was what was intended in the classical definition of a benefice as the right to receive the income from ecclesiastical property *(ex bonis ecclesiasticis)*.[25]

Gradually, however, the generosity of the faithful in Catholic countries either failed or took other trends so that this form of endowment in real property diminished more and more as time went on. On the other hand, in non-Catholic countries or in countries of mixed religion, although the faithful were generous enough in contributing to the support of their priests, still their generosity did not assume the form of constituting a special endowment whence a benefice could be erected. Accordingly, what with the accepted concept of endowment required for a benefice, and the actual lack of such endowments, very few benefices were to be found in these countries, and the clerics who performed the duties of the pastoral office did not consider them-

24 Reiffenstuel, lib. III, tit. V, n. 10-12; Coronata, *Institutiones Iuris Canonici*, II, n. 972.

25 Schmalzgrueber, lib. III, tit. V, n. 2; Reiffenstuel, lib. III, tit. V, n. 6.

selves as beneficiaries. In consequence, they did not consider themselves as bound by the obligation of beneficiaries.[26]

In view of what has just been stated concerning the concept of endowment for a benefice before the Code, it must be concluded that the Code in canon 1410 has greatly enlarged that notion so as to include as canonical endowments many items that formerly were not considered as such. Thus, the number of canonical benefices was either increased, or doubt was removed concerning the beneficial status of many already existing offices which had some right to the receipt of revenue connected therewith. Any cleric, therefore, upon whom is conferred by competent ecclesiastical authority a sacred office to which is annexed the right to revenue from any of the five sources enumerated in canon 1410, provided that this source be declared to constitute the endowment of that office, must hereafter consider himself as the incumbent of a true benefice, and subject to the rights and obligations of beneficiaries.

No longer, in the light of canon 1410, can it be stated that only immovable property actually possessed by the benefice itself as a moral person can make up the endowment of a canonical benefice. True, such property was, and still is, the preferred source of revenue; but it no longer is the only source. Over and above this property actually possessed by the benefice itself, the endowment for a benefice can be constituted by definite obligatory payments of some family or moral person, by the definite voluntary offerings of the faithful, which at the time of the erection of the benefice still remain in their possession, by so-called stole fees received according to and within the limits of diocesan taxation or legitimate custom, and, finally, by choir distributions, one-third of which are to be excluded from being beneficial revenue if the entire revenue of the benefice consists of choral distributions, so that it may yield only to those who are actually present at the choir services and the divine offices.[27]

26 Vidal, "Il Nuovo Codice di Diritto Canonico," — *Civiltà Cattolica* (Roma, 1850 —), LIX (1918), 310-312.

27 Canon 1410. Dotem beneficii constituunt sive bona quorum proprietas est penes ipsum ens iuridicum, sive certae et debitae praestationes alicuius

The Code has introduced this change in the requirements for a canonical endowment in order to keep abreast of the times and of present economic conditions. It is a well known fact that much of the property which was once possessed by benefices, parochial benefices in particular, has since been confiscated by civil governments. Italy offers a striking example of this truth. This confiscation remained uncondoned until a Concordat intervened between the Church and the Italian State in 1929. The pension which the State now pays to pastors constitutes the endowment, in part at least, of their benefice, although the property which formerly pertained to the benefices themselves remains under the dominion of the State. Vidal (1867-1938), however, justly it would seem, demonstrates how these pensions can still be considered as coming from ecclesiastical property in the sense explained above *(ex bonis ecclesiasticis)*.[28]

According to his explanation, these pensions are obtained because of a real pledge *(hypotheca)* which has been placed upon this property whence the revenue is to be derived. With this real obligation attached to it, this property has been *ceded* by the Church to the State. This real obligation upon the property is sufficient to place the revenue derived therefrom in the realm of ecclesiastical property, for the Code defines ecclesiastical property as all temporal property, corporeal (movable and immovable) and incorporeal, real and personal, which belongs either to the Universal Church, or to the Apostolic See, or to individual ecclesiastical moral persons.[29]

Long before the Code the juridical practice of the Sacred Congregations and Tribunals had come to consider these pensions paid by civil governments as sufficient to constitute the endowment of a benefice. Thus, the Sacred Penitentiary, asked whether the salaries which were paid by the Belgian Government

familiae vel personae moralis, sive certae et voluntariae fidelium oblationes quae ad beneficii rectorem spectent, sive iura, ut dicitur, stolae intra fines taxationis dioecesanae vel legitimae consuetudinis, sive chorales distributiones, exclusa tertia earundem parte, si omnes reditus beneficii choralibus distributionibus constent.

28 "Il Codice di Diritto Canonico," — *Civiltà Cattolica,* LIX (1918), 312.

29 Canon 1497, § 1.

to pastors and canons assumed the nature of benefices or of ecclesiastical property, with the consequent canonical effects if such be the case, answered in the affirmative to both queries.[30] The Sacred Congregation of the Council gave a similar decision.[31]

It is, therefore, no longer necessary that the property whence the endowment is derived be in the actual possession or even ownership of the moral person. Indeed, the Code even allows the erection of parishes and quasi-parishes when a fitting endowment cannot be had, provided that it is foreseen that the necessities of the benefice and of the beneficiary are prudently provided for from some other source.[32]

Canon 1410 enumerates the various sources whence an endowment for a benefice may be obtained. It does not, however, necessarily follow that each of these sources is or can be utilized in establishing that endowment. That is to say, the enumeration in canon 1410 must be accepted in a *disjunctive,* not in a *conjunctive* sense. In order that any or all of the sources of revenue enumerated in canon 1410 be actually set aside to constitute the endowment of some particular benefice, a positive definition of a competent ecclesiastical superior must intervene. In each case one must examine the decree for the erection of the benefice to see just which of these sources has been utilized in constituting the endowment.[33] Only in the absence of goods actually possessed by the benefice should the definite obligatory payments of some family or moral person, the voluntary offerings of the faithful, or stole fees be utilized in constituting the endowment of a benefice.[34] It must be remembered that the purpose of a benefice is not to enrich its incumbent, but to provide for him in the exercise of his office a fitting and decent livelihood. Consequently, only

30 S. Poenit. Ap., 19 ian. 1819 — *Thesaurus Resolutionum Sacrae Congregationis Concilii* (167 vols., Romae, 1718-1908), CXXXIII, 506-514.

31 S. C. C. *Carcasson.*, 22 aug. 1874 — *Thes. Resol.*, CXXXIII, 506-514.

32 Canon 1415, § 3.

33 De Meester, *Juris Canonici et Juris Canonico-Civilis Compendium*, III, n. 1393.

34 Vromant, *De Bonis Ecclesiae Temporalibus* (Louvain: Desbarax, 1927), n. 24.

that which is necessary for this purpose should be set aside as constituting the income of the same.

To sum up in a few words what has already been stated, one may well assert with Coronata that four things are necessary for the constitution of an ecclesiastical benefice.[35] Of these four, two are to be considered as its constituent elements; the remaining two are the essential conditions to be observed in its foundation. The two constituent elements are, first, the sacred office, and, secondly, the right to receive the revenue from the endowment attached thereto. The essential conditions are, first, that the benefice be erected as a moral person by competent ecclesiastical authority, and, secondly, that there be present at least an objective perpetuity whereby the benefice of itself, once founded, will not cease to be, but will only at intervals be vacated.

Article 2. The Application of the Elements of a Benefice to a Canonical Parish

As stated at the beginning of this chapter, the inquiry into the nature and the elements of a benefice is not intended here to constitute an end unto itself, but rather has been made with the sole purpose of applying these elements to a canonical parish in order thereby to demonstrate that, since these elements are also to be found in a parish, parishes are and must be considered as benefices. It remains, therefore, but to compare the elements of a benefice with the elements of a parish. To realize this end it will be necessary to re-state these elements as given above, one by one, applying each in its turn as a test to the status of a canonical parish.

a. *The Parish Is a Juridical Entity.* A parish, too, must be considered as a juridical entity or moral person, for a parish, like a benefice, is capable of exercising rights, discharging obligations, vindicating its rights, contracting debts, etc. Only a person, however, whether physical or moral, can engage in functions such as these. Now it stands to reason that a parish is not a physical person; yet, it is also a matter of fact that parishes do exercise

35 *Institutiones Iuris Canonici,* II, n. 972.

rights, discharge obligations, vindicate their rights, and contract debts. The conclusion must necessarily follow, therefore, that a parish is a moral person.

A further indication of the moral personality of parishes can be deduced from the arrangement of the Code itself. Title XXV of the Code, which is worded *"De beneficiis ecclesiasticis,"* treats *"ex professo"* of parishes. But in canon 99 benefices are given as an example of non-collegiate moral persons. In order, therefore, to treat promiscuously of benefices and parishes within the same title, it must be concluded that parishes have the same legal nature as benefices, that is to say, that they, too, are considered by the Code as non-collegiate moral persons.

b. *Establishment or Erection of a Parish.* In accord with what has already been stated, the concept of establishment implies that in the erection of a benefice a positive act on the part of the competent superior must intervene. A mere suggestion or proposal is not sufficient for the establishment of a benefice. With regard to parishes, however, the necessity of this act of positive intervention cannot be postulated *a priori* as flowing from the Code itself in canon 1418 until it has first been proved that parishes are in reality benefices. To establish that proof is the express purpose of this chapter. Certainly, once that fact has been ascertained and accepted, the necessity of an act of positive intervention on the part of a competent superior becomes evident from the Code, for canon 1418 expressly requires that the erection of benefices be effected by a legal document, which shall define the place where the benefice is erected, and describe the endowment of the benefice and the rights and obligations of the beneficiary. It would be a simple matter, therefore, to prove the necessity of positive intervention on the part of a competent superior, provided that parishes are admittedly benefices. But until that has been proved — and again it is stressed that the furnishing of that proof is the purpose and task of this chapter — the appeal to canon 1418 at this point would be tantamount to begging the question. Accordingly, another point of view must be assumed to establish the necessity of this act of positive intervention.

It will be pointed out shortly, and can be presumed here for the moment, that a parish contains within itself a sacred office in the strict acceptation of the term. An office in the strict sense of the term is a "stable position created either by divine or ecclesiastical law, conferred according to the rules of the sacred canons, and entailing some participation at least in ecclesiastical power, whether of orders or of jurisdiction." [36] As a matter of fact, the office of pastor entails the exercise of the power both of orders and of jurisdiction. And it has been pointed out that the stability in a parish is founded not in the person of the pastor himself, but in the parochial office. The power of orders is enjoyed by the pastor in virtue of his ordination to the priesthood; it is not thus, however, with regard to the power of jurisdiction which he exercises in the internal forum, both sacramental and extra-sacramental. There are within the Church two ultimate sources of jurisdiction, both of divine institution, viz.: the office of the Roman Pontiff and the offiice of a bishop. From which of these sources does a pastor obtain his jurisdiction in the internal forum?

Title VIII of the Code reads thus: "Of the Episcopal Jurisdiction and Those Participating in It." [37] Within the confines of this title the Code includes its legislation on pastors. Apparently, therefore, pastors participate in the power of the Episcopacy. As stated above, a pastor does not enjoy the power of jurisdiction in the internal forum by reason of his ordination. Granted, therefore, that a pastor participates in episcopal power, there are two ways in which he can obtain this power. The power of jurisdiction can be communicated to him personally, as is the case with assistants *(vicarii cooperatores)*; this is delegated jurisdiction. The power of jurisdiction can also be communicated by conferring an ecclesiastical office to which this jurisdiction is attached. The jurisdiction granted in such a fashion is ordinary jurisdiction.[38]

36 Woywod, *A Practical Commentary on the Code of Canon Law,* I, 60; canon 145, § 1.

37 Woywod, *op. cit.,* I, 117; *C. I. C.,* Titulus VIII: De potestate espiscopali deque iis qui de eadem participant.

38 Cf. canon 197, §§ 1, 2.

It is ordinary jurisdiction, then, which is enjoyed by a pastor. To attach such jurisdiction to a particular office, however, requires a special act of the bishop whereby the care of souls along with this jurisdiction in the internal forum is established to be committed to some particular priest who has already by reason of his ordination the power of orders. In this manner the office of pastor is created. No mere suggestion on the part of another will suffice; the bishop must intervene by some positive act in the form of a decree for the erection of the parish. Wherefore, if a benefice for its canonical erection postulates a positive act of intervention on the part of a competent superior, so, too, a similar act must intervene for the erection of a parish.

c. *Perpetuity of a Parish.* It has already been established that a benefice in order to be a canonical benefice no longer postulates the need of the concomitant element of subjective perpetuity; it may be present, but it is not required.[39] All that is required is that the benefice enjoy objective perpetuity, that is to say, it must possess that perpetuity which is proper to any moral person.[40]

A parish, however, has been proved to be a moral person. Therefore, a parish, too, enjoys at least objective perpetuity. Moreover, like a benefice, it may at times have the additional note of subjective perpetuity when the incumbent is an irremovable pastor. Subjective perpetuity, however, is not required; objective perpetuity will suffice. And a parish as a moral person *does* enjoy objective perpetuity.

d. *The Ecclesiastical Authority Competent to Erect a Parish.* According to the preceding commentary, a benefice must be erected by competent *ecclesiastical* authority, since it contains within itself the exercise of a sacred office which, as sacred, is reserved to ecclesiastical competence alone.[41] But the office of pastor likewise connotes the exercise of a sacred office in the strict sense of the term. Therefore, a parish, too, must be erected by competent *ecclesiastical* authority.

39 *Supra,* p. 25.

40 Canon 102, § 1.

41 *Supra,* p. 26.

e. *The Office of Pastor Is a Sacred Office.* There seems to be but little need to delay in proving that the office of pastor is a sacred office in the strict sense of the term. An office in this sense has already been defined.[42] The requirements for the first part of the definition have already been established as present in a canonical parish. Moreover, there can be no doubt that a pastor exercises both the power of orders and the power of jurisdiction. The Code legislates at great length concerning the rights and obligations which are proper to the pastor in exercising his priestly orders and his jurisdiction in the internal forum.[43] It follows, therefore, that a parish does contain the exercise of a sacred office in the strict acceptance of the term.

f. *The Right to Revenue Contained in a Parish.* Canon 1410 asserts that stole fees within the limits of diocesan taxation or legitimate custom can constitute the endowment of a benefice. Moreover, canon 463 reserves to the pastor the right to receive the offerings established by approved custom or legitimate taxation in accordance with the provision of canon 1507, § 1. Hence, it must be concluded that the pastor has the right to the revenue accruing to him from the exercise of his office. All that is required is that the pastor have the right to receive the stole fees. It is not essential that he actually receive them. Indeed, they may be so insufficient as to compel the maintenance of the pastor from other sources. Thus, there can exist parishes in which the voluntary offerings of the faithful together with the stole fees are to such an extent insufficient for the fitting maintenance of the pastor that his actual salary is supplied from diocesan funds. But even this state of affairs is contemplated and permitted by the Code, for in canon 1415, § 3, it is expressly stated that it is not forbidden to erect parishes or quasi-parishes in which a proper endowment cannot be had, if one can prudently foresee that the necessary revenue will be obtained from other sources. Therefore, as a benefice to its incumbent, so, too, a parish conveys

42 Canon 145, § 1. *Supra*, p. 26.

43 E. g., canons 738, §§ 1, 2; 802; 845; 848, § 1; 871; 873; 938, §§ 1, 2; 1094.

to its pastor the right to the revenues from the exercise of his office.

With regard to the right which a pastor enjoys to the revenues accruing to him from the exercise of his office some difficulty may be encountered in comprehending how our American parishes can be conceived of as benefices. Do our pastors enjoy this right? Can it be correctly stated that they have the right to assured and voluntary offerings made by the faithful? The writer is inclined to agree with Golden in stating that they do enjoy this right.[44]

> The certain and voluntary offerings of the faithful in this country come in the form of pew rents, block collections, yearly dues, Christmas and Easter collections and the like. We have said that pastors here receive, not these certain and voluntary offerings in their entirety, but stated salaries *(honoraria)*, and that the salaries are considered as the amount of beneficial revenue necessary for their decent support, either with or without living expenses, according as to how the salary is regulated. Can we say then that the pastors here receive the revenue of the parish or benefice? It seems to the writer that we can, and that the circumstances of the country permit the bishops to determine just how much revenue the pastor needs, in harmony with the long standing custom of determining the salary. Even if one must concede that the disposition of superfluous goods must be permitted the beneficiaries without any interference from their bishop, is it not rather the present system that must be changed, than that we conclude that parishes are not benefices? [45]

g. *The Endowment of a Parish.* It has already been pointed out just what is considered by the Code to constitute the endowment of a benefice. History demonstrates how the parochial office has for centuries had attached to it the right to the revenue from the property or real estate annexed to the office.[46] Salaries paid by civil governments to pastors have been interpreted as the

44 Golden, *Parochial Benefices in the New Code,* The Catholic University of America Canon Law Studies, n. 10 (Washington, D. C.: The Catholic University of America, 1925), pp. 103-104.

45 Golden, *Parochial Benefices in the New Code,* p. 104.

46 *Supra,* p. 21.

endowment of their benefice.[47] That voluntary offerings made by the faithful together with the tendered stole fees have been attributed to pastors as of right is a matter of common knowledge, and the Code itself has reserved the right to stole fees to the pastor.[48] It must be concluded, therefore, that if property owned by the benefice itself, or if definite obligatory payments of some family or moral person, or definite voluntary offerings of the faithful, and so-called stole fees can be found attached to a benefice, they can also be found attached to the pastoral office.

In the foregoing pages the nature and elements of a benefice were examined in rather lengthy detail. These elements were then studied in their relation to a canonical parish, and it was ascertained that the same elements are common to benefices and to parishes. The writer, therefore, feels that this state of affairs necessitates and proves the following conclusion. An ecclesiastical benefice is a juridical entity, permanently constituted or erected by competent ecclesiastical authority, consisting of a sacred office and the right to receive the revenue accruing from the endowment of such an office.[49] But a canonical parish is likewise a juridical entity, permanently constituted or erected by competent ecclesiastical authority, consisting of a sacred office and the right to receive the revenue accruing from the endowment of such an office. Therefore, a canonical parish is a benefice.

Article 3. Further Indications That Parishes Are Benefices

A further proof that canonical parishes are considered by the Code as benefices can be drawn from the so-called *argumentum ex convenientia*. If it be supposed, merely for the sake of argument, that canonical parishes are not benefices, where in the Code will legislation concerning parishes be found? It is true that canon 1415, § 3, contains an apparent exception for the erection of parishes which have *not* a sufficient revenue. But

47 S. C. C. *Carcasson*, 22 aug. 1874 — *Thes. Resol.*, CXXXIII, 506-514.
48 Canon 463.
49 Canon 1409.

where can be found legislation concerning parishes which *are* canonical parishes, and *do* meet the requirements of a sufficient revenue, if parishes are not benefices? It is likewise true that canon 216 treats explicitly of parishes, but it explains merely the nature of parishes. So, too, canon 471 concerns itself with the appointment of parochial vicars in the event of the union of parishes with religious houses, with a capitular church, or with some other moral person.

These canons do not, however, concern the actual erection, administration, division, suppression, etc., of parishes. Yet, these items are of the utmost importance in the proper regulation of a diocese. If parishes are not benefices and hence are not included under the laws governing benefices, then where shall such legislation be found? Can it be rightfully supposed that in the Code there is tolerated a *"lacuna"* in the law in a matter of such importance, directly concerning the welfare of souls? Most certainly such an assumption seems unwarranted. From this and other indications in the Code, and particularly in view of the similar juridical condition of parishes and benefices, it must therefore be concluded that the Code intends to include, and, as a matter of fact does include, parishes under its legislation on benefices. Wherefore, parishes are benefices.

Moreover, Title XXV of the Code is worded: *"De beneficiis ecclesiasticis."* Yet, within this title parishes are treated *"ex professo."* Can it be reasonably presumed that the legislator who is so meticulous elsewhere in the Code in proffering a logical development of ecclesiastical discipline, has in this title committed the unpardonable error of treating of two institutes of an entirely different juridical nature under the same identical title? Or is it not rather eminently within reason to admit that when the legislator treats of parishes and benefices under the same title, *"De beneficiis ecclesiasticis,"* that he considers parishes as benefices?

The foregoing are what may be considered as intrinsic arguments derived from the text of the law itself. To these can be added the extrinsic authority of renowned commentators of Canon Law. Certainly, there never was entertained a reasonable doubt containing a denial that the vast majority of European parishes were benefices. True, when the pastors of these parishes were not irremovable pastors, or when the endowment consisted of salaries paid by civil governments, or of voluntary offerings made by the faithful, some doubt was entertained as to the beneficial status of such parishes.[50] But in the light of the Code, which in canons 1409-1410 has precluded the necessity of subjective perpetuity and has so enlarged the notion of an endowment that it is connoted by the actual *status quo* of all existing canonical parishes, these doubts can no longer be entertained.

Wherefore, the vast majority of present-day commentators do not hesitate to accept the common opinion whereby all canonical parishes are considered as benefices. This is admitted even for countries such as the United States of America, Ireland, Australia, England and Wales, where the sole support of the beneficiary is derived in most cases from the voluntary offerings of the faithful or from so-called stole fees.[51]

Finally, attention must be called to the letter of the Apostolic Delegate in 1921 to the Bishops of the United States. In that letter the Delegate quotes Cardinal Gasparri, then the President of the Commission for the Authentic Interpretation of the Code of Canon Law, as answering his queries concerning the canonical status of parishes in the United States by asserting that a parish is always an ecclesiastical benefice.[52]

It is not the writer's intention to demonstrate just how the conclusion is reached that American, Irish, Australian, and English parishes, in which conclusion are comprised all other parishes of a similar status, must in reality be considered as ecclesiastical benefices. The fact that such is the case is merely stated, and

50 Cf. Vidal, "Il Nuovo Codice di Diritto Canonico,"—*Civiltà Cattolica*, LIX (1918), 309-310.

51 Augustine, *A Commentary on the New Code of Canon Law* (8 vols., St. Louis: B. Herder Book Co., 1921-1924), VI, 495; Vermeersch-Creusen, *Epitome*, II, n. 743; Augustine, *The Canonical and Civil Status of Catholic Parishes in the United States*, pp. 84-85.

52 The entire text of this letter can be found in Bouscaren, *Canon Law Digest* (2 vols. [Vol. I—1934; Vol. II—1943], Milwaukee: The Bruce Publishing Company, 1934-1943), I, 149-151.

reference is given to authors who treat the question in detail.[53]

It can be stated, therefore, by way of conclusion to the present chapter, that, since parishes are benefices, whatever is asserted in the Code concerning the union of benefices can, in like manner, be applied to the union of parishes, unless there be an express exception to the contrary, or unless the legal context demand a different application.

53 For the condition of American parishes as benefices, cf. Golden, *Parochial Benefices in the New Code,* pp. 103-106; for the situation in Ireland, cf. Kinane, "The Obligation of Parish Priests to Apply Their Superfluous Revenues to the Poor and to Pious Uses," — *Irish Ecclesiastical Record* (Dublin, 1864 —), 5 series (1913 —), XXVIII (1926), 639-642; for England and Wales, cf. McReavy, "Parochial Benefices in England and Wales," — *The Clergy Review* (London, 1931 —), XV (1938), 189-202; XV (1938), 376; 468-470; 562-564; XVI (1939), 84-88; 275-280; for Australia, cf. Nevin, "Are Parishes in Australia Benefices?" — *Australasian Catholic Record* (Manly, 1923 —), VII (1930), 172-174.

CHAPTER III

THE VARIOUS KINDS OF UNION OF BENEFICES AND THEIR JURIDICAL EFFECTS

Canon 1419. Unio beneficiorum est:

1°. *Extinctiva*, cum aut ex suppressis duobus vel pluribus beneficiis novum atque unicum beneficium efficitur, aut unum vel plura ita alii uniuntur ut esse desinant;

2°. *Aeque principalis*, cum unita beneficia remanent prout sunt, neque alterum alteri subiicitur;

3°. *Minus principalis*, seu per *subjectionem* vel *accessionem*, cum beneficia remanent, sed unum aut plura alii tanquam accessorium principali subiiciuntur.

Article 1. The Various Kinds of Union

Section 1. Notion and Definition of the Union of Benefices

It will serve a useful purpose to recall to mind at the very beginning of this chapter that the writer has already established the fact that parishes are benefices in order that he may justly apply to parishes in particular whatever is stated in the Code concerning the union of benefices in general.[1] Canon 1419, which establishes the various kinds of union of benefices in general, affords an instance of the manner in which the legislation for parishes in particular must be drawn from the legislation regarding benefices in general.

It will also prove helpful to note at this point that practically all the legislation contained in the Code concerning the union of benefices is in the main a re-statement of the old law. Accordingly, those canons which re-state former laws in their entirety must be interpreted in accordance with the old law, and

[1] *Supra*, p. 38.

hence, the interpretations accepted by approved authors are to be followed in the interpretation of these laws in the Code.[2]

There is to be found in the Code of Canon Law no particular canon which affords a generic notion of what is to be understood by the union of benefices. The Code seems rather to presuppose this notion as already known when in canon 1419 it proceeds immediately to establish the various types of the union of benefices. Practically all authors, however, agree substantially in defining the union of benefices as "a joining of two or more juridical entities (benefices), made by competent authority for reasons, and with due observance of the formalities prescribed by ecclesiastical law."[3]

The union of benefices, though permitted by law, is an exceptional procedure. As an exception, therefore, it is considered in law os *odious*,[4] and must be subjected to a strict interpretation.[5] Accordingly, if there be any doubt whatsoever as to whether a union of benefices has in reality been effected, the doubt must be solved in favor of the former and divided status of the benefices, for the presumption must be that a union of the benefices in question has not been accomplished.

Section 2. The Types of Union of Benefices in the Decree of Gratian

The text of Gratian itself nowhere treats of the different kinds of union. The *Glossa Ordinaria* of Joannes Teutonicus (+ 1245), however, does contain a classification of the union of

[2] Canon 6, 2°.

[3] Augustine, *The Canonical and Civil Status of Catholic Parishes in the United States*, p. 137; De Angelis (1824-1881), *Praelectiones Iuris Canonici* (5 vols., Romae, 1908), lib. III, tit. V, n. 25; Santi (1830-1885), *Praelectiones Iuris Canonici* (ed. 4, 3 vols., Romae, 1903-1905), lib. III, tit. V, n. 89; Pistocchi, *De Re Beneficiali*, p. 65; Cocchi, *Commentarium in Codicem Iuris Canonici*, III, n. 92.

[4] Sanguinetti (1829-1893), *Iuris Ecclesiastici Privati Institutiones* (Romae, 1884), p. 370; Ferrari (+ 1874), *Summa Institutionum Canonicarum* (3. ed., 2 vols., Januae, 1887), II, 213.

[5] Canon 19. Leges quae . . . exceptionem a lege continent, strictae subsunt interpretationi.

benefices equivalent in substance to that found in canon 1419.[6] According to this Gloss, the union of churches can be effected in various ways. First of all, they can be united after such a manner that one is subject to the other, so that, by way of example, after such a union rights of eminence and claims of dignity will attach solely to one of the churches.[7]

In the second place, two churches can be so united as to form one church; wherefore, no longer can there be said to exist two distinct churches, but one alone now remains.[8] The Glossator then goes on to point out that a distinction must be made in the type of union just mentioned, known as the extinctive union, for it can be conceived of as taking place in either of two ways. Either both benefices concerned in the union cease to exist as distinct entities and *together* form one entirely new juridical entity, or, secondly, one surrenders its juridical existence and is united to another already existing benefice which continues its existence.[9]

The distinction offered by this Gloss is of the greatest importance, for, as shall be seen presently, the juridical effects of the union differ in accordance with which of these two forms of the extinctive union has been utilized. Indeed, this very distinction of the Glossator has been recognized and preserved by the Code of Canon Law.[10]

A third and final type of union is realized when the episcopal

6 *Decretum Gratiani emendatum et notationibus illustratum una cum glossis* (2 vols., Romae, 1582), *Glos. Ord.*, c. 48, C. XVI, q. 1, s.v. *unire.*

7 "Dico quod variis modis possunt uniri ecclesiae, vel hoc modo ut una subjiciatur alteri: et secundum hoc dignitas erit in una tantum."—*Glos. Ord., loc. cit.*

8 "Vel hoc modo possunt uniri, ut ex duabus dignitatibus una fiat dignitas: et secundum hoc non dicuntur esse duae ecclesiae, sed una tantum." —*Glos. Ord., loc. cit.*

9 "In tali unione distinguendum credo, quod aut ecclesiae simul uniuntur, aut una earum unitur reliquae; quod duo sunt penitus diversa."—*Glos. Ord., loc. cit.*

10 Canon 1419. Extinctiva [est unio] cum aut ex suppressis duobus vel pluribus beneficiis novum atque unicum beneficium efficitur, aut unum vel plura ita alii uniuntur ut esse desinant; canon 1420. In unione extinctiva, beneficio quod *emergit* aut *remanet* . . . etc.

churches are united after such a fashion that both remain as they were before the union, that is to say, episcopal churches, even though by reason of the union one and the same bishop now presides over both. Wherefore, if originally the two episcopal churches were subject to different metropolitans, the same state of affairs continues after as before the union, so that neither metropolitan suffers any loss in his rights in consequence of the effected union.[11]

It has already been stated that this threefold classification of the union of benefices is nowhere to be found in the text of Gratian in the form of a law or canon. From this fact, however, it would be incorrect to conclude that the doctrine itself was unknown at that time. Indeed, although the doctrine in the form of a law or canon is wanting in Gratian, there are other texts which proffer *examples* of the union of benefices for proving conclusively that the doctrine was already known and accepted at a very early date. It will be useful, therefore, to cite these various examples.

After many cities had been so depopulated, among them the locality of Tre Taverne in Italy, that they could no longer have a bishop of their own, and there remained no hope of repairing their churches, Pope Gregory I in the year 592 ordered John, Bishop of Velletri, in addition to his own diocese, to assume the government of Tre Taverne.[12] This text is patently an example of a mutually co-ordinative union.

Similarly there is in Gratian another example of the union of benefices in which it is worth quoting the text itself to illustrate the manner in which what is now called the mutually co-ordinative union was conceived of at that time.

[11] "Tertio modo possunt uniri ecclesiae: puta quod utraque remaneat episcopalis. Et secundum hoc remanent duo episcopatus, licet idem sit episcopus utriusque ecclesiae: secundum hoc si primo suberant istae ecclesiae diversis metropolitanis, propter illam unionem neuter metropolitanus perdit ius suum."—*Glos. Ord.*, c. 48, C. XVI, q. 1, s.v. *unire*.

[12] C. 49, C. XVI, q. 1; Jaffé, *Regesta Pontificum Romanorum ab condita Ecclesia ad annum post Christum natum MCXCVIII* (ed. 2., correctam et auctam auspiciis Gulielmi Wattenbach curaverunt S. Loewenfeld, F. Kaltenbrunner, P. Ewald, 2 tomes in 1 vol., Lipsiae, 1885-1888), n. 1202.

The clergy and people of Terracina, where their Bishop, Peter, had died, asked of Pope Gregory I that Agnellus, Bishop of Fondi, be given also to them as their bishop. Pope Gregory in the year 592 granted their request in a letter to Agnellus, specifying in what manner the union was to be understood:[13]

> Illud quoque fraternitatem tuam scire necesse est, quoniam sic praedictae Terracinensis ecclesiae cardinalem esse constitutimus sacerdotem ut et Fundensis Ecclesiae pontifex esse *non desinas;* nec curam gubernationemque eius praetereas: quia ita fraternitatem tuam saepe dictae Terracinensis ecclesiae, sicuti praefati sumus, praesse praecipimus ut antedictae Fundensis ecclesiae tibi iura potestatemque nullo modo subtrahamus.[14]

The plurality of benefices had already been forbidden at this time.[15] The Glossator, therefore, anticipating a forthcoming objection on this score, proceeded to show how the Bishop of Fondi could assume the government of the diocese of Terracina, and still retain that of Fondi. He answered the objection by stating that the union of benefices constituted an exception to the general law of the Church which forbade a plurality of benefices.[16] Referring to the word *subtrahamus,*[17] the Glossator stated that unless the phrase "nullo modo" had been inserted, then just as soon as Agnellus received the second episcopate he would automatically have lost the first.[18]

[13] It is impossible to determine from the text whether this union was a temporary or a perpetual union. In either case, however, the reason for quoting the text here is justified, since it demonstrates the effects of a mutually co-ordinative union, and these effects were the same whether the union was perpetual or merely temporary.

[14] C. 6, C. XXI, q. 1; Jaffé, *Regesta Pontificum Romanorum,* n. 1217.

[15] "Singuli ecclesiastici iuris officia singulis quibuscumque personis singulatim committi iubemus. . . . Sicut enim varietas membrorum per diversa officia et robur corporis servat et pulchritudinem representat, ita varietas personarum per diversa nihilominus officia distributa et fortitudinem et venustatem sanctae ecclesiae manifestat."—c. 1, D. LXXXIX.

[16] *Glos. Ord.,* c. 6, C. XXI, q. 1, s.v. *desinas; also,* c. 17, C. 7, q. 1.

[17] *Glos. Ord.,* c. 6, C. XXI, q. 1, s.v. *subtrahamus.*

[18] "Si quis iam translatus est ab alia ecclesia in aliam, nihil habet commune cum priori ecclesia."—c. 3, C. XXI, q. 2.

These texts from Gratian do not exemplify precisely the union of parishes. They do, however, exemplify the union of benefices in general. Accordingly, whatever is stated concerning the union of benefices in general can justly be applied to the union of parishes. Hence, it can be concluded that the doctrine of the union of parishes as contained in canon 1419 was already prevalent at the time of Gregory the Great (590-604). Indeed, canon 5 of the Council of Sardica (343) implies the same discipline at least by indirection, when the refusal of a bishop to consecrate another in the event he was the sole remaining bishop was severely reprimanded. The underlying reason was in all likelihood the same as that which later forbade the simultaneous holding of several bishoprics.

Section 3. The Types of Union in the Decretals

Like the Decree of Gratian, so also the Decretals have nothing explicit in the text itself concerning the union of benefices. The only matter traceable in the Decretals is to be found in a Gloss to a decretal which was issued by Innocent III in the year 1206.[19] The matter in this Gloss is substantially the same as, and indeed almost identical with, the matter of the Gloss of Gratian referred above. Hence, it would be of no purpose to repeat it here. It is sufficient to note that the Glossator of the Decretals carried over into his commentary the very same doctrine as that which earlier was taught by the Glossator of Gratian.[20]

19 *Glos. Ord.*, c. 1, X, *Ne sede vacante*, III, 9; *Quinque Compilationes Antiquae nec non Collectio canorum Lipsiensis* (ad librorum manu scriptorum fidem recognovit et adnotatione critica instruxit Aemelius Friedberg, Lipsiae, 1882), Comp. III, lib. 3, tit. 9, c. un.; Potthast, *Regesta Pontificum Romanorum* (2 vols., Berolini, 1874-1875), n. 2714.

20 Hostiensis *(Commentaria in Quinque Decretalium Libros*, [5 vols. in 3, Venetiis, 1581], in c. 1, X, *Ne sede vacante*, III, 9), one of the foremost of all Decretalists, maintained that there were *five* ways of uniting benefices, despite the fact that the ancient writers had distinguished but three. This five-fold division of Hostiensis, however, in no way contradicts the three-fold classification of earlier canonists. It is a lengthier division, but

Section 4. The Types of Union According to Pre-Code Authors

In relation to the union of benefices canon 1419 distinguishes the various possible kinds of union into three classes: the extinctive, the mutually co-ordinative, and the relatively subordinative union of benefices. There is, however, an even more fundamental distinction whence the division of the Code is derived. Practically all Pre-Code authors derived the types of union from a two-fold source: the *real* or *personal,* and the *temporary* or *perpetual* union of benefices.[21]

A *real* union is one in which the benefices themselves undergo a change. The union, therefore, affects the very essence of the benefices. A *strictly personal* union, on the other hand, is one in which the essence of the benefices remains intact; the status of the beneficiary alone is changed. That is to say, in a *strictly personal* union the benefices themselves remain as they were before the union, divided and independent one of the other. But, whereas before the union they had been held by several clerics, now, precisely because of the union, they are held by a single incumbent. Technically considered, therefore, a personal union is more of the nature of a unification in the number of beneficiaries than it is of the nature of a union of the benefices themselves.

It is to be noted that the writer uses the words "strictly personal," and this not without good reason. Unless the term "personal" be qualified, the whole foundation for the distinction between *real* and *personal* unions would be wanting. The very concept of the union of benefices, whether the essence of the benefices be affected or not, postulates their conferment upon but one single person. Otherwise, there would be no point to

it contains nothing that is not already contained in the aforementioned three-fold classification. The same doctrine of Hostiensis can also be found in his *Summa Aurea* (Lugduni, 1568), lib. III, *Ne Sede Vacante,* § *Quot modis,* n. 5.

21 Reiffenstuel, lib. III, tit. XII, nn. 37-38; Sanguineti, *Iuris Ecclesiastici Privati Institutiones,* p. 370; Ferrari, *Summa Institutionum Canonicarum,* II, 213; Lombardi, *Iuris Canonici Privati Institutiones* (ed. 2., 3 vols., Romae, 1910), II, 359.

uniting the benefices. From this point of view, therefore, any or all forms of the union of benefices whatsoever must of necessity be *personal.* When, however, the term *"strictly personal"* is used, that type of union is intended in which the essence of the benefices remains intact. In this fashion the writer wishes to distinguish a strictly personal union from a *real* union, the latter being a personal union only in the wider sense of the term, and a union in which the essence of the benefices themselves is affected.

A *temporary* union is one which is made for the life of the incumbent of the united benefices. A *perpetual* union, on the other hand, is one which prescinds from the life span of the incumbent. The classifications of the union of benefices as real or personal, and as temporary or perpetual, are not, however, mutually exclusive. That is to say, the classification is not so precise as to require that the union be either real or personal, temporary or perpetual, or conversely, never both real and temporal, or personal and at the same time perpetual. There is between these classifications an interdependence.

As a real union can be in theory, though scarcely ever is in practice, either temporary or perpetual, so too a strictly personal union can be either temporary or perpetual. If the sole purpose of the union is to favor the incumbent *(intuitu personae),* then the union is a *temporary* personal union. But if, on the contrary, the union, though strictly personal, has in view the welfare not of the incumbent as such, but rather of the benefices themselves and thereby of the Church as a whole *(intuitu Ecclesiae),* then such a union is considered as a *perpetually* personal union.

It is the *temporary* personal union, therefore, rather than the union of benefices, that is classified as connoting a tacit dispensation from the law which forbids a plurality of incompatible benefices.[22] A *perpetually* personal union, on the other hand, since it favors the welfare of the benefices themselves, can be classified as a true union of benefices. Wherefore, a mutually

22 Canon 1439, §§ 1, 2.

co-ordinative union, which is nothing other than a perpetually personal union, is enumerated in canon 1419 among the true types of the union of benefices.

Of these two forms of union, namely, the temporary personal and the perpetually personal, the latter is by far the less odious in law. Wherefore, should a doubt arise as to whether the temporary personal or the perpetually personal union was intended by the superior who effected the union, the presumption must be in favor of the perpetually personal union, for when the contrary is not apparent, the Church rather than an individual is to be favored.[23]

This conclusion may, at first glance, appear rather strange. It could appear that a temporary personal union rather than a perpetually personal union would be more favorable to the Church, since upon the death of the possessory incumbent, the benefices themselves would once more return to the free and separate disposition of the ecclesiastical superior.

In making a decision in a doubtful case, however, that form of union is to be preferred which favors the Church rather than the individual cleric. It must be remembered that a temporary personal union, according to the definition, is one which is effected in favor of a determined person, whereas a perpetually personal union, according to its definition, prescinds from the advantages accruing to the individual, and considers solely the welfare of the benefices themselves, and thereby the welfare of the entire Church. Accordingly, the conclusion, though it may occasion surprise, is nonetheless evidently justified.

Reiffenstuel (1641-1703) offered some rules which could be followed in practice if there was to be made a decision whether the union was to be understood as temporary or perpetual.[24] A personal union is only then to be understood as temporary when it is evident that the superior intended to favor some definite person. If, on the contrary, it appears, even if only doubtfully so, that the superior intended to favor the Church as a whole, then the union is to be considered as perpetual. Likewise, the

23 Reiffenstuel, lib. III, tit. XII, n. 38.

24 Lib. III, tit. XII, n. 37.

union must be interpreted as perpetual whenever apart from a specific limitation to the contrary it is effected according to the will of the Holy See *(ad beneplacitum Sanctae Sedis)*, for since the Holy See as a moral person will of itself endure, so too the union will continue in effect until it be recalled by the Holy See. In the meantime, it must be considered as a perpetual union.

The Code of Canon Law makes no explicit mention of the classification of the union of benefices into real or personal, temporary or perpetual. These types of union are, however, contained *substantially* in the legislation of the Code, for the so-called extinctive union as well as the relatively subordinative are nothing other than a *real* union of benefices, while, as was stated above, the mutually co-ordinative form of union is a *perpetually personal* union.

No mention is made of the temporary personal union except in a negative way. When the Code forbids a plurality of incompatible benefices it effectively removes this form of union from the scope of competence of inferior legislators. Certainly, the Holy See which is empowered to make exceptions to its own laws can, if it so desires, effect a temporary personal union. An action of this kind is, however, reserved to the Holy See itself.

It seems to be of rather great importance to stress the fact that the doctrine of the pre-Code authors is still to be found within the legislation of the Code, implicitly though it be, for in view of this fact the presumptions of the old law can still be followed for the solving of all doubtful questions concerning the union of benefices.[25]

Section 5. The Types of Union in the Code of Canon Law

Canon 1419 enumerates the types of union known in modern legislation. They are respectively, the extinctive, the mutually co-ordinative, and the relatively subordinative union of benefices. It is, indeed, interesting to note that the inclusion of these types of union in canon 1419 marks the first time that such a

[25] Canon 6, 2°.

classification has ever found its way into the *text* of any compilation or collection of ecclesiastical legislation.

The writer does not wish, however, to imply by this statement that the doctrine itself is new, or that it is proper to the Code alone, for, as was shown in the preceeding sections of the present article, legislators and commentators have for centuries utilized this very classification. What the writer does intend to stress is that in the Code, for the first time, this classification is stated in the form of a law or regulation with its definite place in an authentic collection of canons.

Canon 1419 is concerned exclusively with perpetual unions. These are *real* unions if they are comprised under the class of extinctive or subordinative unions, but *strictly personal* unions if they belong to the class of co-ordinative unions.

a. *The Extinctive Union.* A union of benefices is extinctive when out of two or more benefices a new single benefice is created, or when one or several benefices are united to another in such a manner that they cease to exist.[26] These words of canon 1419 immediately recall to mind the distinction afforded by the Glossator of Gratian which has already been related.[27] Substantially they include that very distinction.

The extinctive union, also called a union by means of *commergence (per confusionem)* can take place in two ways. First, out of two benefices an entirely new benefice may be created. The resulting benefice is neither the one nor the other of the original benefices, but a new moral person. It is true, of course, that the resultant benefice appropriates its nature, its qualities, its privileges, etc., from the benefices out of which it was formed. There is, however, no communication, as it were, of moral personality. The new benefice is as much a new moral person as a child procreated by its father and mother is a new and distinct physical person. Nothing whatever remains of the moral personality of the antecedent benefices. An entirely new and distinct moral person has come into existence as the direct result of the extinctive union.

26 Canon 1419, 1°.

27 *Supra*, p. 44.

The second form of the extinctive union is that wherein one or more benefices, previously in existence, are now so united with another pre-existing benefice that they cease to exist; the latter benefice, however, continues its existence. This second form of the extinctive union differs from the first in that not *all* the antecedent benefices thereby lose their moral personality. The benefice or benefices that are united with the other do lose their personality; but the benefice augmented by the transaction retains its moral personality, and becomes the inherent subject for the rights and obligations which formerly pertained to the benefices which have now become extinct as a result of the union. There is, however, no formation of a new moral person in this second form of the extinctive union, as is to be found in the first form.

The first form is contemplated by the Code when it describes an extinctive union as one in which out of two or more suppressed benefices a new and single benefice is created.[28] The second form is described by the Code as that in which one or more benefices are united with another in such a fashion that they cease to exist.[29]

Paragraph 1 of canon 1420 in like manner clearly indicates the existence of two forms of the extinctive union when it distinguishes between the benefice which *emerges* and the benefice which *remains*.[30] In this canon the word *emergit* patently contemplates the first form of the extinctive union; the word *remanet*, on the other hand, connotes a definite reference to its second form.

It seems expedient to illustrate these two forms of the extinctive union by way of a practical example. Let it be supposed that for reasons established by law and through authoriza-

28 Canon 1419, 1°. Unio beneficiorum est: 1°. *Extinctiva* cum . . . ex suppressis duobus vel pluribus beneficiis novum atque unicum beneficium efficitur. . . .

29 Canon 1419, 1°. Unio beneficiorum est: 1°. *Extinctiva* cum . . . unum vel plura ita alii uniuntur ut esse desinant.

30 Canon 1420, § 1. In unione extinctiva, beneficio quod *emergit* aut *remanet*. . . . (Italics inserted by the writer.)

tion accorded by competent authority an extinctive union is effected between two parishes: the parish of St. John and that of St. Mary. If these two parishes are united in such a manner that subsequent to their union a new parish known as St. Stephen's is created, then the first form of the extinctive union was employed for the completion of the transaction. Both the parish of St. John and the parish of St. Mary cease to exist as moral persons, and a new moral person, the parish of St. Stephen, has come into existence. But if, on the contrary, the parish of St. Mary is so united with that of St. John that, following the union, St. Mary's is no longer a distinct moral person, whereas St. John's continues to exist, but in an augmented state, then it must be stated that the second form of the extinctive union was utilized.

Among all the possible forms of union, the extinctive union is by far the most odious in law, for if the original condition of benefices is so jealously guarded as to render odious in law any form of modification of the same, it goes without saying that the process whereby the benefice is not only modified but extinguished in its entirety must be considered as the most odious form of all. It is for this reason that the effecting of extinctive unions is reserved to the exclusive competence of the Holy See.[31] Accordingly, the extinctive union of benefices, parishes in particular, though theoretically possible, is none the less seldom employed in practice.

b. *The Co-ordinative Union.* A union is mutually co-ordinative when the united benefices remain as they are, neither one being subjected to the other.[32] According to the distinction offered above,[33] the co-ordinative union is a personal rather than a real union, for the essence of the benefices themselves is in no way affected. Only the condition or status of the beneficiary is altered by such a union; the essence of each benefice remains precisely what it was before the union.[34]

31 Canon 1422.

32 Canon 1419, 2°. *Aeque pricipalis,* cum unita beneficia remanent prout sunt, neque alterum alteri subiicitur.

33 *Supra,* pp. 48-49.

34 Coronata, *Institutiones Iuris Canonici,* II, n. 980.

Of all possible modes for the union of benefices the mutually co-ordinative is the least odious in law.[35] The reason for this assertion is to be found in the fact that, though the co-ordinative union confers a new status upon the benefices, nonetheless no intrinsic change whatsoever is effected in their essence. Hence, should a doubt arise as to whether the union was intended as a co-ordinative union, as an extinctive union, or as a subordinative union, then the presumption must favor the co-ordinative form of union as the least odious of all.

The co-ordinative form of union is sometimes also called a merely *subjective* union. It is termed so not because it is effected in favor of a determined person *(intuitu personae)*, for then it would be a temporary personal and not a co-ordinative union at all, as described by the Code in canon 1419, 2°; it is called *subjective* precisely for the reason that the union affects only the incumbent of the united benefices, prescinding from the advantages accruing to the same, the while the benefices themselves remain as before, independent one of the other.

In present day juridical practice the co-ordinative form of union is generally encountered with reference to the administration of dioceses. Dioceses, therefore, afford the most common opportunity for the application of this form of union. It can, however, be equally well employed with reference to parishes.

As an example of what has just been stated, the writer suggests a situation in which the ordinary of a large diocese is faced with a lamentable paucity of priests who can act as pastors for the parishes of his diocese. If such be in reality the case, then the writer is inclined to believe that the form of the *co-ordinative* union of parishes in the various districts throughout the diocese may serve as the happiest solution for properly consulting the extant needs. No extraordinary procedure would be necessitated in the case, for the Code expressly states that it is within the competence of the local ordinary to effect a mutually co-ordinative union among parishes.[36]

35 Santi, *Praelectiones Iuris Canonici*, lib. III, tit. V, n. 93; Pistocchi, *De Re Beneficiali*, p. 67.

36 Canon 1423, § 1.

A solution such as this cannot be called impracticable on the score that according to canon 1423, § 3, all unions made by the ordinary must be perpetual. Although it is true that all unions effected by the bishop must be made in perpetuity, still there is nothing to prevent him from disbanding the extant union by restoring the two parishes to two separate incumbents in accord with the provision of canon 1427.

c. *The Subordinative Union.* The union of benefices is of a subordinative character or by way of *subjection* or *accession,* when the various benefices remain, but one or more are subordinated to another as accessory to the principal benefice.[37] The accessory follows the principal benefice upon which it is dependent,[38] so that the cleric who obtains the principal benefice by that very fact becomes invested also with the accessory, and is accordingly bound to comply with the obligations arising from both benefices.

The Code states explicitly that in a subordinative union all the benefices *remain.*[39] Accordingly, no conclusion can be reached other than that the benefices continue in existence as distinct moral persons, though one be subjected to the other. There seems to be a discrepancy, however, between the law of the Code and the doctrine of not a few renowned pre-Code authors. Indeed, Augustine does not hesitate to assert that because of the word *remanent* a new construction of the former doctrine is apparently to be admitted.[40]

37 Canon 1419, 3°. *Minus principalis* est unio, seu per *subjectionem* vel *accessionem,* cum beneficia remanent, sed unum aut plura alii tanquam accessorium pricipali subiiciuntur. (Italics inserted by the writer.)

38 "Accessorium naturam sequi congruit principalis." — Reg. 42, R. J., in VI°.

39 Canon 1419, 3°. *Minus principalis* . . . cum beneficia *remanent.* (Italics inserted by the writer.)

40 "This appears like a new construction of the former doctrine. For if we understand the commentators of the Decretals aright, it was maintained that the accessory benefice was changed in its status to such a degree that it ceased to be a distinct entity, and was considered part and parcel of the principal benefice."—*The Canonical and Civil Status of Catholic Parishes in the United States,* p. 139.

It cannot be denied that unanimity among pre-Code authors was wanting with regard to this particular point. Reiffenstuel unequivocally stated that in the accessory or subordinative union the status and nature of the united benefice was changed to such a degree that, whereas previously it was an ecclesiastical benefice, existing by itself, it ceased to be such by reason of the aforementioned union, and became a part of the other with which it was united. Because of this, he continued, the united benefice *ceased to be a benefice,* lost the name of a benefice, and appropriated unto itself the nature of the benefice with which it was united.[41] Reiffenstuel did not stand alone in his assertions upon this matter. Among others, Garcia[42] and Fagnanus (1598-1678)[43] had propounded a similar doctrine.

But if it be true that there were eminent canonists who maintained that following upon a subordinative union the accessory benefice ceased to exist as a benefice, it is also true that there were authors of equal importance who advanced the contrary opinion. Thus, while admitting a radical change in the status of the accessory benefice, Schmalzgrueber contented himself with establishing this change as a *quasi-extinction.*[44] Pirhing (1606-1679) at an earlier date,[45] and De Angelis (1824-1881)[46]

41 "Per hanc accessoriam unionem mutatur status et natura beneficii uniti, adeo, ut licet antea fuerit ecclesiasticum beneficium per se substistens, per unionem praedictam desinat esse talis, et fiat pars alterius cui unitum fuerit. . . . Et hac ratione, beneficium unitum mediante unione desinit esse beneficium, atque amittit nomen beneficii; et inducit naturam alterius, cui unitur et accrescit."—lib. III, tit. XII, n. 45.

42 *De Beneficiis Ecclesiasticis,* pars XII, cap. II, n. 12.

43 *Commentaria Super Quinque Libros Decretalium* (5 vols., Romae, 1661), lib. I, tit. VII, n. 31.

44 "Per eam unionem minus principalem beneficium sic unitum quasi extinguatur, quia assumit naturam, qualitates et privilegia beneficii principalis, cui adhaeret."—lib. III, tit. V, n. 153.

45 *Jus Canonicum in Quinque Libros Decretalium Distributum* (5 vols., Dilingae, 1722), lib. III, tit. V, n. 202.

46 *Praelectiones Iuris Canonici,* lib. III, tit. V, n. 25.

together with Santi (1830-1885) at the end of the last century,[47] appear to have taken a similar position.

One must admit, therefore, that there is some foundation for Augustine's statement that the commentators of the Decretals maintained that the accessory benefice was changed in its status to such a degree that it ceased to be a benefice or a distinct entity.[48] In view, however, of the contrary opinion of other Decretalists, it may appear that Augustine's statement is too sweeping in its contention.

Ordinary prudence would counsel singular caution in taking exception to such renowned authors as Garcia, Fagnanus, and Reiffenstuel. And yet, with all the respect due their opinion, the writer feels himself constrained to disagree with their doctrine and adhere rather to the contrary opinion of Pirhing, Schmalzgrueber, De Angelis and Santi.

In the opinion of the former, the accessory benefice upon the execution of the subordinative union ceased to exist as a benefice. But if their doctrine was correct, then what difference was there between the subordinative union and the extinctive union in its second form? In both cases the united benefices would have ceased to exist as benefices or juridical entities in their entirety. What, therefore, if their opinion were followed, was the foundation for the distinction between the subordinative and the extinctive union?

In the light of the law of the Code, however, regardless of the nature of the doctrine on the part of the Pre-Code authors, one must maintain that in a subordinative union both benefices remain as juridical entities, though the one be subjected to the other as a direct consequence of such a union.[49]

47 "Per hanc unionem cessat titulus beneficii seu Ecclesiae inferioris et habetur ceu *pars* alterius cui accessorie unitur."—*Praelectiones Juris Canonici,* lib. III, tit. V, n. 92.

48 Augustine, *op. cit.,* p. 139.

49 Canon 1419, 3°. *Minus principalis* . . . cum beneficia *remanent.* (Italics inserted by the writer.)

Article 2. The Juridical Effects of the Various Types of Union

Section 1. The Juridical Effects of the Extinctive Union

Canon 1420, § 1. In unione extinctiva, beneficio quod emergit aut remanet, omnia iura et onera extinctorum competunt, et, si inter se componi nequeant, meliora ac favorabiliora.

In the extinctive union the benefice which emerges or remains has all the rights and obligations of the extinct benefices; and if these rights and obligations be incompatible the better and more favorable rights and obligations are to be retained.

". . . *beneficio quod emergit aut remanet*. . ." The word *emergit* has reference to that form of the extinctive union wherein both benefices coalesce to form a new benefice. The word *remanet*, on the other hand, connotes the extinction of one benefice by reason of its union with another already existing benefice which then continues in its existence as a benefice, but in an augmented form.

If for the uniting of two parishes the first form of the extinctive union is used *(beneficium emergit)*, a new appointment of a pastor must be made by the ordinary.[50] The question whether one of the two former pastors is to be invested with the pastoral office in the new parish will be investigated later when consideration is given to the rights of the actual incumbents at the time the union is effected.[51] Since, however, a new parish is the result of this first type of the extinctive union, neither of the two former pastors becomes *its* pastor by reason of his previous appointment. Unless, therefore, a new appointment of a pastor be made, all acts of jurisdiction on the part of the one who continues as the incumbent would be invalid. Accordingly, the assisting at marriages and the hearing of confessions on the part of the unappointed incumbent would be invalid if the necessary author-

50 Canons 147, § 1; 152.

51 *Infra*, p. 135.

ization and requisite jurisdiction for these acts were made to derive solely from the possession of the ordinary power which inheres in the office of a pastor when he has been rightfully installed in office. If, however, the conditions enumerated in canon 209 were actually present, the Church would supply the lacking jurisdiction. Moreover, a new profession of faith would be required from the incumbent of the new parish.[52]

On the contrary, in the second form of the extinctive union *(beneficium quod remanet)*, no new appointment of a pastor would be necessary, for in this form the fact of extinction can be predicated only for that parish which is being united with another already existing parish. The pastor of that parish with which another is united would continue as pastor of the augmented parish. No new profession of faith would be required of him, since no new benefice has been conferred.

What has been stated concerning pastors in this regard is likewise to be applied to the assistants *(vicarii cooperatores)* actually assigned to the parish at the time the extinctive union was effected. Wherefore, if the union was effected according to the first form of extinctive union, the appointments of the assistants would automatically cease, and a new appointment would be necessary should the service of these assistants be required for the newly formed parish. But if, on the other hand, the extinctive union were effected in the second form, then only the assistants of the parish which became extinct by reason of the union would automatically cease to function. The assistant assigned to the parish augmented by the union would continue in the capacity of assistant.

"... *iura* ..." In either form of the extinctive union, all the rights which previously pertained to each separate benefice coalesce in the benefice which emerges as well as in the benefice which perdures. These rights may be either of the spiritual or of the temporal order.

[52] Canon 1406, 7°. Coram loci Ordinario eiusve delegato, Vicarius Generalis, *parochi* et ii quibus provisum fuit de beneficiis quibusvis, etiam manualibus, curam animarum habentibus. . . . (Italics inserted by the writer.)

The parochial functions and rights reserved by the Code to pastors are founded upon the parochial office with which he is invested.[53] These functions are, moreover, exercised with regard to the parishioners or those who have acquired a domicile or quasi-domicile within the parish, or who are *vagi* actually within the parish limits, or those, finally, who have nothing more than a diocesan domicile or quasi-domicile and are now within the limits of the parish.[54] As a direct consequence of the union of two parishes, therefore, these parochial functions and rights are now exercised by the pastor with reference to a greater number of parishioners.

All the privileges which formerly pertained to each of the parishes concerned in the union are likewise to be transferred to the new parish resulting from the extinctive union. Thus, it may occur that of these two parishes one had the privilege of Daily Exposition of the Blessed Sacrament, the other the privilege of Midnight Mass on certain feasts of the year. Accordingly, the parish emerging or remaining from the extinctive union would then enjoy both privileges.

All temporal rights of both parishes are likewise to be transferred to the new parish. Wherefore, the right to the revenue from the endowment of what formerly had been two separate benefices, now as a consequence of the union becomes the right of but one beneficiary alone. To the incumbent of this single benefice must be attributed the right to receive the stipend from any or all founded Masses which pertained to the two former parishes.[55]

The title to all real property which pertained to both parishes, such as the church itself, the convent, the rectory, or the school, must be vested in the new parish, and provision must be made to guarantee the right to this title before the civil law. Should, however, the multiplicity of identical parish buildings necessitate the disposal of one or the other, then the rules for

[53] Canons 462, 463.

[54] Canon 94, §§ 2, 3.

[55] Cf. canon 826, § 3.

the alienation of church property must be strictly adhered to.[56] Moreover, that parish church which is perhaps no longer serviceable cannot be converted to profane uses except in accord with the provisions of canon 1187.

". . . *et onera* . . ." As the rights, so too the obligations of both parishes are to be transferred to the single parish resulting from an extinctive union. If, therefore, as stated above, the parochial functions and rights reserved to a pastor are multiplied with reference to a greater number of parishioners who now pertain to the parish, correspondingly it must be maintained that the pastor's obligations towards the needs of his parishioners are likewise multiplied.

All temporal debts and obligations which formerly burdened both parishes as separate entities are now to be assumed and discharged by the single parish which emerges or remains after the extinctive union. Insomuch, however, as the extinctive union is affected by way of *commergence (per confusionem)*, the credits of one parish and the possible debits of the other are to be amalgamated to discharge the obligations of the remaining single parish. If both parishes had no credits but only debits, then all the debits of both parishes are to be assumed by the new single parish which then becomes responsible for payment.

The parish records and archives which according to canon 470, §§ 1-4, formerly pertained to each individual parish, subsequently to the union are to be transferred to the new parish and entrusted to its care. These are to be kept as *distinct* records with reference to the time preceeding the union. Following the union, however, all baptism, confirmation, marriage and death records are to be recorded in a new *single* set of records as pertaining to but one parish.

It has already been stated that following an extinctive union the right to the stipends from the founded Masses of both parishes becomes proper to the new pastor. With this right is concomitant the obligation placed upon the pastor to satisfy such obligations. The pastor of the new parish, however, is bound to offer but one official Mass for his flock on the days established in

[56] Cf. canons 1530-1532.

canon 339, § 1, for the obligation to celebrate the official Mass for his flock is placed upon a pastor by reason of the parochial office which he holds. Following the union, however, the incumbent is invested with but one parochial office. Accordingly, there is but one obligation to offer the official Mass for his flock.

". . . *et si inter se componi nequeant* . . ." These words of canon 1420, § 1, indicate that a conflict may at times arise between the rights and obligations of one parish and those of the other when an extinctive union is effected. Such a conflict is, indeed, possible, and arises from the fact that the rights and obligations have been transferred to but one single parish, to be exercised by but one single pastor.

". . . *meliora ac favorabiliora* . . ." These words afford a key to the solution of any conflict that may arise between the rights and obligations of the parishes concerned in an extinctive union. Should such a conflict arise, then there will attach to the newly created or also quantitatively augmented parochial benefice those rights and obligations which prove to be the more advantageous and favorable with regard not only to the parish itself but also to its pastoral incumbent. To prevent any doubt in this matter, the superior who effects the union should determine at the time of the union itself just which rights and obligations are to be assumed by the new or augmented parish.[57]

The solution offered by these words of the canon is in full conformity with the provision of the old law.[58] The *meliora* of the text are such as affect the spiritual and the temporal elements of the benefice itself.[59] Thus, divine worship should not be curtailed, insofar as it does not conflict with parochial duties. Strict duties, however, prevail.[60] In the proper adaptation and settlement of the temporal rights and obligations those which in their administration give promise of greater security and lessened

57 Blat, *Commentarium Textus Codicis Iuris Canonici* (5 vols. in 6, Romae: ex Typographia Pontificia in Instituto Pii IX, 1921-1927), III (1923), pars altera, n. 139.

58 Cf. c. 14, C. XXXII, q. 1; c. 48, 49, C. XVI, q. 1.

59 Blat, *Commentarium, loc. cit.*

60 Augustine, *The Canonical and Civil Status of Catholic Parishes in the United States,* p. 138.

encumbrance are to be preferred. Thus, investments which command a higher rate of interest at the risk, however, of a fully certified revenue will be relinquished for investments which command a lower rate of interest, but yield their income in a completely assured manner. Likewise, outstanding obligations on which the pro-rated payments entail greater encumbrances will be exchanged for such as make lesser demands as long as the benefit of the parish is equally served thereby.

By the *favoribiliora* are to be understood those rights and obligations which are more favorable to the incumbent of the benefice. Thus, by way of example, if an exempt and a non-exempt parish are united by way of an extinctive union, the resulting parish must be entitled to the privilege of exemption. Since, however, the Holy See alone is competent in this form of union, one can look to the apostolic rescript to ascertain the precise juridical effects decided upon in a particular case. In the lack of such specification, however, one should apply the principle mentioned above.

Section 2. The Juridical Effects of the Co-ordinative Union

Canon 1420, § 2. In [unione] aeque principali, quodlibet beneficium conservat suam naturam, iura et onera, sed, vi peractae unionis, uni eidemque clerico unitorum beneficiorum tituli conferri debet.

In the co-ordinative union each benefice preserves its nature, rights, and obligations, but in virtue of the effected union the titles of the various united benefices must be conferred upon one and the same cleric. With reference to parishes, therefore, it must be stated that subsequent to the co-ordinative union each parish remains precisely what it was before the union. By virtue of the union a certain communication is established with reference only to the *person* of the pastor, not with reference to the parishes themselves.

"... *conservat* ..." This word of canon 1420, § 2, implies that the nature, rights and obligations of the parishes must already have been established previous to the union, for that which did not already exist cannot be *conserved.* The union, therefore, neither bestows nor changes the nature, rights and obligations of these juridical entities. It merely conserves them in that state in which they already existed previous to the union.

"*. . . naturam . . .*" Benefices are, by their nature, distinguished as consistorial or non-consistorial, as secular or religious, as residential or non-residential, as manual or perpetual, and as entrusted or not entrusted with the care of souls.[61] They may also be exempt or non-exempt, and conferrable by the Ordinary according to an unrestricted right of disposition or subject to another's right of patronage.[62] The nature in which a benefice will be vested is determined at the time of its establishment. When later it may be found necessary or useful to unite several of these benefices, they continue to retain after the union the same identical nature that was theirs previous to the union.

Wherefore, what was a secular or a religious benefice prior to the union will continue to be secular or religious subsequent to the union. The only change effected by the union consists in this, that whereas before the union a religious was the incumbent of the religious benefice and a secular held the secular parish, subsequent to the union *either* a religious *or* a secular, but not both, becomes the pastor of both parishes. It remains for the Holy See, which alone is competent to effect the union of a religious with a secular parish, to determine the type of cleric who shall become the pastor of both parishes.[63]

What has been said concerning the union of a secular with a religious parish is applicable in like manner to other parishes of a different nature. Thus, should an exempt parish be co-ordinatively united with a non-exempt parish, each parish will remain afterwards with reference to its nature precisely what it was before the union.

What has been stated is in theory true. But it appears that in *practice* there are two exceptions to the statement of the Code that subsequent to a co-ordinative union each benefice retains the nature which it had before the union.

61 Canon 1411, 1°-5°.

62 Canon 1424.

63 Canon 1422.

In the first place, if a parish which has for its pastor a removable incumbent is united by means of a co-ordinative union with a parish which has for its pastor an irremovable incumbent, then in theory for the duration of the union each parish would retain its ertswhile status. But in practice the more ample prerogative attaches to both parishes through the unified office of the one pastor who rules over both parishes, and hence, in relation to the canonical causes and the administrative procedure for the incumbent's removal or transfer, there must be applied those prescriptions of law which regulate these matters with respect to an irremovable pastor.[64]

The causes and the procedure for the removal or transfer of a removable pastor differ somewhat from those prescribed for the same procedure in the case of an irremovable pastor. Yet, as long as the union endures, the pastor cannot be removed or transferred from the one of these parishes independently of the other, so that he would be removed as the removable pastor of the one the while he continues as the irremovable pastor of the other. Since his removal from one parish necessarily implies his removal from the other in view of the effected union of the two parishes, it is evident that his removal can be effected only in the manner specified by law for the removal of an irremovable pastor. The removal from the one parish apart from the simultaneous removal from the other parish would, if the possibility of this were admitted, be tantamount to the dissolving of the effected union.[65]

In theory and principle the rule is not waived, but in practice and application this rule cannot abstract from the fact, coincidental though it be, that for the duration of the effected union one and the same pastor holds an indivisible incumbency in the two parishes. To effect his removal from the one there must necessarily be employed the means which suffice for his removal from both. But, to effect his removal from both it is necessary also that he be removed in his capacity of an irremovable pastor. Therefore, the act of his removal essentially postulates the em-

[64] Cf. canons 2147-2161.

[65] Schmalzgrueber, lib. III, tit. V, n. 158.

ployment of the procedure which relates to an irremovable pastor.

The second exception to the principle established in canon 1420, § 2, whereby both benefices retain the nature that was theirs previous to the co-ordinative union seems to arise in the case wherein a parish subject to the unrestricted disposal *(liberae collationis)* of the bishop is united with one to which the right of patronage is attached *(iuris patronatus)*. The Code states that, if with the consent of the patron the church or benefice is united with another not subject to the right of patronage, then the right of patronage is extinguished.[66] In such a case the appointment of the one incumbent to both parishes becomes freely conferable through the Ordinary. The two parishes, therefore, cannot be said to retain the same nature which they had before the union.

". . . *iura* . . ." Following upon the co-ordinative union of two parishes, each parish retains its proper rights and privileges. There is to be no intercommunication of these rights and privileges as is the case in the extinctive union. Wherefore, should one parish have the privilege of daily Exposition of the Blessed Sacrament, and the other the privilege of Midnight Mass, each parish retains its particular privilege even after the union, but neither parish can borrow from or appropriate the privilege of the other.

The revenue or income of each parish is to be received and administered independently one of the other. The credits of one parish, therefore, cannot be used in payment of the debits of the other. The property owned by each of the parishes is to be employed for the exclusive welfare of that parish to which it pertains. Finally, the pastor receives the right to the stipend from the founded Masses of each of the parishes concerned in the co-ordinative union.

". . . *et onera* . . ." Each parish must continue to discharge its own proper obligations. The one parish cannot make use of the goods of the other parish which is united with it by way of a co-ordinative union. Separate books are to be kept by the pastor, and separate reports are to be submitted to the Ordinary

66 Canon 1470, 5°.

each year.[67] Should the obligations and duties be multiplied in a co-ordinative union to such an extent that they cannot be discharged by the pastor alone, then the situation can be remedied by the appointment of an assistant *(vicarius cooperator)* in accord with the prescriptions of canon 476, §§ 1-5.

A pastor, however, who governs two or more parishes which are co-ordinatively united is bound on the days listed in canon 339 to celebrate but one official Mass for the people entrusted to his care.[68] This prescription of canon 466, § 2, constitutes a change from the old law.[69] The canon is to be understood in the sense that on one and the same day the pastor is obliged to apply but one official Mass for the different parishioners entrusted to his care. But if the feast of the patron of the place falls upon *different* days in the different parishes, then the pastor has the obligation of applying the official Mass on the festive day of each particular parish.[70]

Finally, the appointment to, the resignation from, and the vacancy in one of the united benefices necessarily implies the presence of the same elements in the other, for the appointment to, the resignation from, and the vacancy in the one apart from the other would of necessity dissolve the union.[71] Since in a mutually co-ordinative union, however, both benefices remain as benefices and both retain their title,[72] similarly both benefices must be considered as truly vacant should their incumbent for any reason cease to function as pastor. Therefore, in any petition for the acquisition of two co-ordinatively united parishes,

67 Canon 1525.

68 Canon 466, § 2. Parochus qui plures forte paroecias aeque principaliter unitas regat . . . unam tantum debet Missam pro populis sibi commissis diebus praescriptis applicare.

69 Vermeersch-Creusen, *Epitome,* I, n. 553; Cocchi, *Commentarium,* II, n. 346; Donnellan, *The Obligation of the Missa Pro Populo,* The Catholic University of America Canon Law Studies, n. 155 (Washington, D. C.: The Catholic University of America Press, 1942), p. 76.

70 S. C. C. *Blesen.,* 12 nov. 1927— *A A S,* XX (1928), 84.

71 Wernz, *Ius Decretalium,* II, n. 273.

72 Canon 1420, § 2. . . . uni eidemque clerico unitorum beneficiorum tituli conferri debent. Cf. also, Schmalzgrueber, lib. III, tit. V, n. 157.

mention of both parishes must be made explicitly, since the petition for the one does not include the petition for the other, each parish having its particular title. Moreover, a canonical appointment must be made to each of the two parishes for the validity of the appointment to either.[73]

Section 3. The Juridical Effects of the Subordinative Union

Canon 1420, § 3. In unione minus principali, beneficium accessorium sequitur principale, ita ut clericus, qui principale obtinet, eo ipso et accessorium consequatur atque utriusque onera implere debeat.

In a subordinative union the accessory benefice follows the principal in such a manner that the cleric who obtains the principal benefice obtains also by that very fact the accessory benefice, and is bound to fulfill the obligations of both benefices.

"*. . . beneficium accessorium sequitur principale . . .*" It has already been demonstrated how in a subordinative union both benefices remain as benefices.[74] The nature of the accessory benefice, however, follows the nature of the principal benefice with which it has been united.[75] Thus, for example, if a non-exempt benefice is subordinatively united with an exempt benefice, then subsequent to the union the accessory benefice also enjoys the privilege of exemption. So, too, if a benefice to which was attached the right of patronage is united with a benefice unrestricted by any such right, the right of the patron is thereby extinguished, since the accessory follows the nature of the principal benefice.[76]

"*. . . ita ut clericus qui principale obtinet, eo ipso et accessorium consequatur . . .*" In a subordinative union the accessory benefice loses its own independent *title,* so that the cleric

[73] Canon 147, § 1.

[74] *Supra,* p. 56.

[75] "Accessorium naturam sequi congruit principalis."—Reg. 42, R. J. in VI°.

[76] Wernz-Vidal, *Ius Canonicum,* II, n. 173; Cocchi *Commentarium,* III, n. 92, p. 215; Vermeersch-Creusen, *Epitome,* II, n. 753. p. 530.

who obtains the principal benefice automatically obtains also the accessory benefice. Unlike the co-ordinative union, mention of both benefices in a request to obtain the principal benefice is not required, but it is understood that the accessory is granted with the principal benefice.

The accessory benefice, moreover, cannot be said to be truly *vacated* upon the death, resignation, or removal of the incumbent of the principal benefice, for a benefice which is no longer *sui iuris* cannot be truly vacated, since it has no title which could be conferred. Since, therefore, the accessory benefice is never truly *vacated* as long as the union endures, all rights of presentation or conferment in regard to the accessory benefice necessarily abate. Moreover, should the law have required some particular personal qualifications of the incumbents of the accessory benefices, then only those qualifications which have been established in respect of the incumbent of the principal benefice are to be exacted, once the union has been executed.[77]

"*. . . atque utriusque onera implere debeat . . .*" The obligations of both benefices remain. The cleric who governs the parishes united by way of a subordinative union is bound to fulfill the obligations of both benefices. Thus he is bound to celebrate, either personally, or through the ministry of another, all the founded Masses of both parishes. As in the co-ordinative union, separate books are to be kept for both parishes, and the funds of both parishes though they may be merged into one common fund must be listed as pertaining to distinct parishes. Thus, should the union be later dissolved, no difficulty will be met in assigning to each parish its due proportion of the common fund.

77 Wernz-Vidal, *Ius Canonicum, loc. cit.;* Coronata, *Institutiones Iuris Canonici,* II, n. 980.

CHAPTER IV

THE INCORPORATION OF PARISHES

Incorporation is still another form of the union of parishes.[1] It is thought proper to explain at the very outset why the writer has chosen to treat of this matter in a separate chapter, instead of including it in the preceding chapter which considered the various types of the union of parishes. Several reasons have influenced this decision. In the first place, canon 1419 treats explicitly of the union of *benefices*. Accordingly, extinctive, co-ordinative, and subordinative unions are concerned primarily with the union of one *benefice* with another *benefice*. Incorporations, on the contrary, are concerned with the union of a benefice with some other *moral person,* whether collegiate or non-collegiate, which, however, is *not a benefice.*[2]

Legislation, therefore, concerning the incorporation of parishes is not to be found except indirectly in canons 1419 and 1420. Canon 1423, § 2, on the one hand, treats both of the forms of incorporation permitted to local ordinaries, and also of the forms which transcend his competence.[3] Canon 1425, §§ 1, 2, on the other hand, treats only of the union of a parish with a religious house. However, although no explicit mention is made of the incorporation of parishes with other moral persons, still, whatever is established concerning canon 1425 can, with the necessary adaptations, be equally applied to all forms of the incorporation of parishes.

The matter to be treated in this chapter is, indeed, extremely complicated and will require a rather lengthy commentary. This

1 The term *incorporation* is to be understood in this work in its canonical sense, not in the sense in which it is employed in American Civil Law.

2 "Incorporatio differt a simplici unione quia uniuntur solum beneficia inter se; incorporantur vero beneficia cum alia etiam persona morali."—Coronata, *Institutiones Iuris Canonici,* II, n. 981, p. 374.

3 The commentary on canon 1423, § 2, is given later in this work. Cf. *infra,* pp. 109-112.

fact, therefore, affords the second and most cogent reason for consigning the matter to a special chapter. The correct interpretation of canon 1425, with its inevitable consequences, is still a matter of controversy. Eminent canonists are to be found in support of contrary opinions. Fully aware of the controversy and its complications, therefore, the writer does not delude himself by believing that the consideration to be given the matter in the following pages will in any way definitely terminate the controversy. He can only examine the arguments advanced by both sides, add his own observations, and adhere to that opinion which seems more in accord with the principles of law.

Before entering upon an examination of the question, however, the writer deems it of the utmost importance to make the following observation. The Holy See enjoys exclusively the right to unite a parish with a religious house. Accordingly, by reason of eminent domain, in executing a union of this kind the Holy See can make of the property of the united parish whatever disposition it may desire to make. It is essential, therefore, that one examine the rescript of incorporation thoroughly in order to ascertain whether *special* juridical effects have been established therein. If so, these and these alone are to be observed. But if the rescript contains no *express* mention of particular effects for a union when it is granted *ad temporalia tantum* or when it is made *pleno iure,* then it seems that the *general* effects indicated in the Code are to be observed.

Article 1. General Notions Concerning the Types of the Incorporation of Parishes

Incorporation has already been defined as the union of a benefice with some other moral person which is not in itself a benefice. It will be useful to recall to mind that in an earlier part of this work it was stated that there are two essential elements in any benefice: the spiritual and the temporal element.[4] It is precisely these two elements that also give rise to the various types of incorporation. An incorporation which is effected

[4] *Supra*, p. 22.

plenissimo iure consists in the transfer to the religious house of both the spiritual and the temporal elements of the united parish in such a way that the parish is entirely removed from the jurisdiction of the local ordinary.[5]

The second form of incorporation of a parish is known as that which is effected *pleno iure*. According to canon 1425, § 2, if the Holy See unites a parish *pleno iure* with a religious house, the parish becomes a religious parish, and the religious superior is permitted to nominate one of his religious subjects to exercise the care of souls. This cleric is called the *vicar* in accord with the provision of canon 471. The right of approbation and institution of this cleric, however, pertains to the local ordinary. Moreover, the vicar is subject to the jurisdiction, correction, and visitation of the local ordinary in matters which pertain to the care of souls.[6]

The third form of incorporation of a parish with a religious house is known as the union which is conceded *ad temporalia tantum*. In this form of union the religious house acquires the right to the *fruits* or *income* of the parish. The religious superior, moreover, obtains the right to *present* to the local ordinary for institution in the parish a secular cleric of his own choice. To this cleric a suitable portion of the income is to be assigned.[7] The spiritual rights of the parish, however, are vested in this secular priest who is truly the pastor of the parish.

Canon 1425, § 1, refers to this secular priest merely as the *sacerdos* presented by the religious superior to the local ordinary. In canon 1423, § 2, it is stated that the bishop is empowered to unite a parish with the cathedral or with a collegiate church situated within the parish limits. This is, indeed, a true form of the incorporation of parishes. Now, as shall be seen later,[8] the more common interpretation of this canon regards the bishop as empowered to effect this incorporation either *ad temporalia tantum* or *pleno iure*. Canon 1423, § 2, further states that a suitable portion of the income in such an event is to be assigned to

5 Cf. Wernz-Vidal, *Ius Canonicum*, II, n. 175, b, p. 196.

6 Canon 631, § 1.

7 Canon 1425, § 1.

8 *Infra*, p. 111.

the pastor *(parochus)* or vicar *(vicarius)*. Canon 471, however, definitely designates the cleric who exercises the care of souls in a parish united *pleno iure* to a moral person as the *vicarius*. Since, therefore, the bishop can execute this form of incorporation in either one of two ways, namely, *ad temporalia tantum* or *pleno iure*, and since in canon 1423, § 2, the word *vicarius* has, in accord with the provision of canon 471, reference to a union which is effected *pleno iure*, it seems that the *parochus* referred to in canon 1423, § 2, denotes the cleric who exercises the care of souls subsequent to a union which is conceded *ad temporalia tantum*. The *sacerdos* mentioned in canon 1425, § 1, therefore, must be interpreted as having the same status as the *parochus* in canon 1423, § 2, even after the union of the parish which is conceded *ad temporalia tantum*.[9]

Finally, parishes may be *entrusted* to religious.[10] In such a case both the spiritual and the temporal rights of the parish remain intact. The only change in the state of a parish *entrusted* to religious consists in this, that because of special circumstances, and with proper authority, a secular parish is by way of exception to the rules of canon 1411, 2°, and 1442 conferred upon a religious cleric instead of upon a secular. It is in this sense that some of our American parishes have been given over to religious. So far as the writer has been able to ascertain, there is no instance in this country of the union of a parish with a religious house which is conceded *ad temporalia tantum*. In the vast majority of cases the religious cleric, and not the religious house as such, is the incumbent of the benefice, and the benefice, though occupied by a religious, remains a secular benefice.[11]

[9] "Propterea per hanc unionem [*ad temporalia tantum*] ecclesia paroecialis non mutat statum . . . atque regitur non per vicarium; sed per parochum *de se* . . . inamovibilem . . ."—Pistocchi, *De Re Beneficiali*, p. 102.

[10] The word *entrusted* is capable in itself of signifying the status of a parish *united* with a religious house (cf. Bastnagel, *The Appointment of Parochial Adjutants and Assistants*, pp. 157-159). To avoid confusion, however, it shall be used in this work in direct contraposition to the word *united*, whether the latter be regarded as connoting either a union which is conceded *ad temporalia tantum*, or a union which is effected *pleno iure*.

[11] For a discussion of the status of parishes in charge of religious in

The notions of the union which is conceded *ad temporalia tantum* or effected *pleno iure* as indicated in canon 1425, §§ 1, 2, are identical with those given by pre-Code authors.[12]

Article 2. The Juridical Effects of the Incorporation of Parishes

It has just been stated that harmony exists between the old law and its commentators and the new law and its commentators in establishing the notion of the incorporation of parishes. With regard to establishing its effects, however, the situation is entirely different, and one is immediately confronted with a two-fold tendency, the tendency of the commentators upon the old law to

this country prior to the Code, cf. Hannan, "The Juridical Status of Parishes of Religious," — *The Jurist* (Washington, D. C., 1941 —), I, 329-335; Dooley, "The Juridical Status of the Parishes of Religious: Another View" — *The Jurist*, III, 117-128. Hannan *(art cit.*, p. 333) maintains that there was no union of these parishes in the canonical sense of the word. Dooley, on the other hand, seems to confuse the issue, for while he states that "all of the parishes in the United States managed by religious clergy are united *pleno iure*" *(art. cit.*, p. 119), still his whole line of argument leads one to conclude that he considers the parishes as merely *entrusted* to religious and not united to their house. Thus, he maintains that the *locum tenens* of each parish is a true canonical pastor *(art. cit.*, p. 128). Were the parish united *pleno iure* with the religious house, however, the religious cleric in charge of the parish would not be a pastor *(parochus)*, but merely a vicar *(vicarius)* in accord with the provision of canon 471, § 1. Moreover, he seems to confuse the Indult required to *entrust* a parish to religious with the Indult required to *unite* a parish with a religious house. The matters are not identical and a special Indult is required for each transaction.

12 "Quod attinet ad parochias unitas et incorporatas, sciendum est, earum quasdam monasteriis unitas esse tantum *quoad temporalia*, quasdam autem *pleno iure*. Unio quoad temporalia tunc censetur facta quando decimae aliique reditus parochiae sunt assignati monasterio, sed ius instituendi rectorem beneficii pertinet ad Episcopum, solo iure *praesentandi* monasterio relicto. . . . Pleno iure dicuntur unitae seu incorporatae quando, praeter ius percipiendi temporales reditus, etiam administratio spiritualium, scilicet curae animarum, in monasterium translata est, atque in tali parochia rector principalis censetur esse abbas monasterii." — Engel, *Collegium Universi Juris Canonici* (9. ed., Beneventi, 1760), lib. III, tit. XXXVII, n. 10; cf. also, Reiffenstuel, lib. III, tit. XXXVII, n. 2.

suppress the incorporated parish as a distinct entity, and the tendency of positive legislation to conserve its juridical status. It becomes necessary, therefore, to propose the following questions. Does the parish even after its incorporation remain as a distinct *subiectum iuris*, capable of possessing its own property? If so, who is to administer its property?

Section 1. The Ownership and Separate Administration of the Property of the Incorporated Parish

a. *Pre-Code Legislation and Pre-Code Authors.* Pre-Code authors classified the incorporation of parishes as a form of the subordinative union. Now, as has been already demonstrated,[13] it was a common teaching that one of the principal effects of a subordinative union consisted in this, that the accessory benefice lost its identity, and became, as it were, engulfed in the principal benefice. Indeed, Giambattista de Luca (1614-1683) likened the accessory benefice to a river flowing into the sea, and being swallowed up therein.[14] Garcia,[15] Reiffenstuel[16] and others proposed a similar doctrine. Thus Aichner (1816-1911) did not hesitate to state that subsequent to the incorporation, not only the *usufruct* of the goods of the incorporated parish, but the dominion thereof was itself transferred to the religious house, so that the incorporated parish ceased to be a *subiectum iuris.*[17]

In direct contrast to this teaching of the commentators, positive ecclesiastical legislation seems to have vindicated the con-

13 *Supra*, p. 57.

14 "Ubi unio est accessoria seu subiectiva (minus principalis), res unita amittit suum nomen et essentiam ac efficitur *membrum* seu praedium ad instar alluvionis seu fluminis intrantis in mare et assumentis naturam ipsius maris, *extincto flumine* cum similibus." — *Theatrum Veritatis et Iustitiae* (15 vols. in 8 and Index, Coloniae Agrippinae, 1706), VIII, *De Praeeminentiis*, disc. 29, n. 9, p. 82. (Italics inserted by writer.)

15 ". . . unio unius beneficii facta alteri accessorie, operatur *extinctionem* et *suppressionem* nominis et tituli beneficii uniti ita ut . . . iudicetur ut praedium eius cui fit unio." — *De Beneficiis*, pars XII, cap. II, n. 12.

16 ". . . beneficium . . . per unionem praedictam desinit esse tale et fit pars alterius, cui accessorie unitum fuit . . . et induit naturam illius cui accrescit." — lib. III, tit. XII, n. 45.

17 *Compendium Juris Ecclesiastici* (6. ed., Brixinae, 1887), p. 274.

tinued existence of the moral personality of the parish even *after* its incorporation. That is to say, it considered the parish as a *subiectum iuris,* capable, therefore, of retaining its goods under its own proper dominion. Moreover, though the parish and the religious house were united, even *pleno iure,* these enactments of the Holy See seem to have required a separate administration of the goods of the parish and of the goods of the religious house.

The Sacred Congregation of the Propagation of the Faith, as noted by Leo XIII (1878-1903) in his Constitution *Romanos Pontifices,* issued an instruction concerning missions in England to the effect that religious were not bound to render an account to the bishop of goods pertaining to the religious as such; they were, however, bound to give an account of the goods given directly to the mission under their care.[18]

Leo XIII in his Constitution *Romanos Pontifices* not only confirmed this Instruction of the Congregation of the Propagation of the Faith, but confirmed also the decrees of the Second Council of Westminster in which an exact determination was made of what was to be understood as given *intuitu personae religiosi,* and as given *intuitu paroeciae vel missionis.* It may be objected that the Constitution was concerned only with parishes *entrusted* to religious and not with such as were *united* with their house. The Constitution, however, seems to deal equally with both. Previous legislation, as mentioned by Leo XIII himself, had stated that the vicar of a parish which was united *ad temporalia tantum* with a monastery was not bound to give an account of the *temporalities* of the parish to the bishop. Leo XIII, however, authoritatively interpreted the word temporalities *(temporalia)* as referring only to the *fruits* or *income* of the parish, not to the goods of the parish as such.[19] By inference,

18 S. C. de Prop. Fide, instr., 19 apr. 1869: "Missionarii regulares bonorum temporalium ad ipsos, qua regulares spectantium, rationem Episcopo reddere non tenentur; eorum tamen bonorum quae missioni, vel regularibus *intuitu missionis* tributa fuerint, Episcopi ius habent ad iisdem missionariis regularibus, aeque ac a parochis cleri saecularibus rationem exigendi." — *Fontes,* n. 582, § 25. (Not included in the *Collectanea.)*

19 Leo XIII, const. *"Romanos Pontifices,"* 8 maii, 1881, § 24: "Neque haec ex eo infirmatur, quod Urbanus II in Concilio Claramontano, aliique

therefore, Leo XIII seems to imply that when a parish is united with a religious house an account of the parish property must be given the bishop. Since, therefore, this Constitution treats of donations which must be attributed to the parish or mission as such, it seems logical to conclude that the parish was considered, even after its union, as a *subiectum iuris*, capable of possessing its own property, and requiring a separate administration of its funds. With these considerations in mind, one can now proceed to explore the legislation of the Code itself.

b. *Legislation of the Code and Post-Code Authors.* Canon 1425, § 1, states that if the Holy See unites a parish *ad temporalia tantum* with a religious house, that religious house acquires the right *only (solummodo)* to the *fruits* or *income (fructus)* of the parish. Wernz-Vidal, however, notwithstanding the express words to the contrary employed in canon 1425, § 1, maintain that in the union of a parish which is conceded *ad temporalia tantum* with a religious house, the very goods *(bona)* of the parish are transferred to the religious house in such a way that the religious house becomes the *subiectum dominii.*[20] Coronata[21] and Cocchi[22] seem to maintain a similar opinion.

post eum Romani Pontifices decreverunt circa Ecclesias parochiales, quoad temporalia monasteriis iunctas, teneri vicarios respondere Episcopis de *plebis cura,* de temporalibus vero non ita, cum monasterio suo sint obnoxii; siquidem . . . certum exploratumque est in iis pontificiis decretis ac litteris appellatione *temporalium,* beneficii *fructus* et quae *beneficiati personae* adhaerent compendia significari." — *Fontes,* n. 582.

20 "Effectus autem incorporationis *minus pleno iure factae* imprimis est translatio *bonorum* temporalium beneficii in domum religiosam, cui incorporatum fuit, tamquam in verum et proprie dictum *subiectum dominii,* salvis oneribus pro sustentatione vicarii vel similibus expensis persolvendis, quae ad instar servitutis bonis incorporatis inhaerent." — *Ius Canonicum,* II, n. 175, b, p. 197. (Italics inserted by the writer.)

21 "Rationem administrationis spiritualis vicarius reddere debet Ordinario loci, rationem vero administrationis *temporalis* Superiori domus religiosae." — *Institutiones Iuris Canonici,* II, n. 981, d, p. 375. (Italics inserted by the writer.)

22 "Quoad incorporationes cum domo religiosa adverte: Si a Sede Apostolica paroecia domui religiosae uniatur *ad temporalia tantum* quod attinet, tunc: a) domus religiosa particeps fit solummodo fructuum seu *bonorum* temporalium paroeciae . . ." — *Commentarium,* III, n. 93, d, p. 216.

Accordingly, they are in harmony with the conception of pre-Code authors in maintaining that subsequent to a union which is conceded *ad temporalia tantum* the parish ceases to be its own *subiectum iuris,* and the religious house assumes this rôle.

It is the contention of the writer, however, that in the light of canon 1425, § 1, this opinion cannot be supported. The canon in no way states that the goods or property itself are transferred to the religious house. On the contrary, it expressly states that only the *fruits* or *revenue (solummodo fructuum)* are transferred to the religious house. Wherefore, the writer fails to understand how it can be contended that in view of canon 1425, § 1, the parish united to a religious house *ad temporalia tantum* ceases to be a *subiectum iuris.* Rather, it seems that the parish as a benefice or moral person retains the ownership or dominion of all the property that pertained to it before such a union was executed. Whereas, however, before the union the fruits or income of the parish were received by a secular beneficiary, now, subsequent to the union which is conceded *ad temporalia tantum* they pertain to the religious house. A suitable portion thereof is to be assigned to the secular priest presented by the religious superior to the local ordinary, and approved by the latter as the one in whose charge rests the care of souls in the parish. Finally, the writer does not stand alone in advancing this opinion. Goyeneche,[23] Blat[24] and Bondini[25] all maintain a similar opinion.

23 "Nunc e contra, mihi videtur, non amplius posse hanc doctrinam (veterum canonistarum et ipsius Wernz-Vidal) sustineri ex novo Codice in quo evidenter paroecia . . . etiam incorporata remanere subjectum dominii cui acquiritur ea bona quae ejusdem paroeciae intuitu donantur . . . Igitur . . . nunc tenendum paroeciam licet incorporatam esse subjectum dominii bonorum paroecialium quae utique pertinent ad collegium vel ad communitatem sed quorum immediatum subjectum est paroecia ipsa." — "Consultationes," *Commentarium pro Religiosis* (from 1935, *Commentarium pro Religiosis et Missionariis,* Romae, 1920 —), X (1929), 40. (Hereafter cited *CpR[M].)*

24 ". . . haec unio (ad temporalia tantum) quoad effectum sic intelligenda est: *Domus* illa *religiosa particeps fit,* quia non omnes fructus illi obveniunt, *solummodo fructuum,* seu temporalium redituum paroeciae." — *Commentarium,* III, pars altera, n. 324. p. 402.

25 "Dunque la chiesa, la dote e quanto altro formava la proprietà della

The juridical status of the parish after it is united with the religious house *ad temporalia tantum* seems then to be this: All the property *(bona)* which prior to the union was under the dominion of the parish continues to be so even after the union, and cannot be amalgamated with the goods of the religious house. Such property includes the parish church, all real estate, and foundations or pious causes pertaining to the parish as such. The usufruct of these goods, however, or the right to the *fruits* or *income* is transferred to the religious house, and can be disposed of at the will of the religious house, since these fruits do come under the dominion of the religious and can be amalgamated with their common goods.

Further support for the opinion that the parish remains a *subiectum iuris* even after it is united *ad temporalia tantum* with a religious house can be found in the Code itself. It is stated that incorporation is a form of the subordinative union.[26] Canon 1419, 3°, however, explicitly states that in a subordinative union the benefices *remain.*[27] Now, it is essential to the nature of a benefice that there be a stable source of income. A parish, however, has been proved to be a benefice. Moreover, the benefice itself is the *subiectum iuris* and has the dominion or ownership of its endowment; the beneficiary has only the usufruct of these goods. How then can it be contended that subsequent to a union which is conceded *ad temporalia tantum* the parish ceases to be a *subiectum iuris,* when the Code expressly states that subsequent to a subordinative union the benefices remain, and when it is known that a benefice to be a benefice must be its own *subiectum iuris?*

Still another indication can be found in the Code itself to sustain the contention of the writer that the legislator considers a parish as a *subiectum iuris* even after it has been united *ad*

parrocchia, non passa al monastero, che ne ha soltanto l'uso e usufrutto . . ." — "Circa il rendiconto del parroco religioso al Vescovo," *Il Monitore Ecclesiastico,* XXXVIII (1926), 343.

26 Pistocchi, *De Re Beneficiali,* p. 93; Vermeersch-Creusen, *Epitome,* II, n. 752, 4°, p. 529; Coronata, *Institutiones Iuris Canonici,* II, n. 981, p. 373.

27 Canon 1419, 3°. *Minus principalis* (est unio) cum beneficia remanent . . .

temporalia tantum or *pleno iure.* Canon 630, § 1, states that a religious who governs a parish, whether with the title of pastor or *vicar,* remains bound to observe his vows and the constitutions insofar as this observance is consistent with his office. Paragraph one of canon 630, therefore, treats of a religious who rules over a parish not only when it is *entrusted* to the religious, but also when it is *united* with the religious house. This is clearly indicated by the use of the words *"sive titulo parochi sive titulo vicarii."* In canon 471 that cleric who exercises the care of souls in a parish which is united *pleno iure* with a religious house, or with some other moral person, is called the *vicarius.* The writer wishes, therefore, to stress the fact that canon 630, § 1, is concerned with the religious who cares for a parish which is *united* with the religious house as well as with the religious who cares for a parish which is merely *entrusted* to a religious house. With this fact in mind, the writer can now proceed to establish his argument.

Paragraph 3 of the same canon 630 states that the goods which a religious vicar or pastor acquires for the parish *(intuitu paroeciae)* are to be considered as acquired by the parish itself. The words *"ipsi paroeciae acquirit"* in canon 630, § 3, clearly indicate, therefore, that the legislator still considers the parish as a *subiectum iuris,* even though it be united with a religious house.[28]

Canon 631, moreover, states that with regard to temporal goods the religious pastor or *vicar* is to be governed by the norms of canon 533, § 1, n. 4. Canon 533, § 1, n. 4, however, states that any religious whatsoever, even a member of an exempt order, is bound to obtain the consent of the local ordinary before investing money which has been given to a parish or mission, or to the religious themselves for the parish or mission *(intuitu paroeciae vel missionis).* Here again the parish is considered as a *subiectum iuris,* capable of acquiring and possessing property in its own name, even though it has been united with a religious house,

[28] "Ex hoc canone (630, § 3) liquet paroeciam *incorporatam* Religioni esse subjectum dominii potestateque frui pergere nedum bona habendi sed et alia acquirendi." — Goyeneche, "Consultationes" — *CpR,* X (1929), 40.

for reference is made to canon 533, § 1, n. 4, by canon 631, § 3, which legislates for *vicars,* that is, for those who in accord with canon 471 govern a parish which is united *pleno iure* with a religious house.[29]

From the foregoing arguments derived from the legislation of the Code, as also from the added testimony of authors, it seems to the writer to be clearly indicated that a parish, even though it be united *ad temporalia tantum* with a religious house, continues to exist as a *subiectum iuris* and retains the ownership of the goods which pertained to it before the union was executed. Can the same opinion be sustained with regard to parishes united *pleno iure* with a religious house? The writer is inclined to answer in the affirmative.

A union which is effected *pleno iure* is nothing other than a combination of the union which is conceded *ad temporalia tantum* plus the union which is granted *ad spiritualia.*[30] The statement that a parish remains a *subiectum iuris* and retains the dominion over its property, therefore, applies equally as well to the union which is effected *pleno iure* as it applies to the union which is conceded *ad temporalia tantum.* Canon 1425, § 1, contains an enumeration of the effects of both types of incorporation. Now, in accord with what has already been stated, canon 1425, § 1, concedes to the religious house with which a parish is united *ad temporalia tantum* only the *fruits* or *income* of the parish. In the opinion of the writer, canon 1425, § 2, in describing a union which is effected *pleno iure* contains nothing which could lead one to conclude that the disposition of the ownership or dominion of the property pertaining to the parish in any way is at all different in this case from the other. The parish itself, therefore, remains the *subiectum dominii* in both types of incorporation.

29 "Idem deducitur ex can. 533, § 1, in quo praecipitur praevius Ordinarii consensus ut religiosus collocet pecuniam datam paroeciae." — Goyeneche, *art. cit., CpR,* X (1929), 40, 177.

30 Iam ergo . . . incorporatio pleno iure id addit quod non solum unio fiat quoad temporalia, sed etiam quoad spiritualia." — Goyeneche, "Consultationes," *CpR,* X (1929), 40.

Canon 1425, § 2, states that in a union which is effected *pleno iure* the parish becomes a religious parish *(paroecia fit religiosa)*. How then are the words *"paroecia fit religiosa"* to be interpreted? Is the phrase *"ecclesia fit religiosa"* to be considered as equivalent in meaning to the phrase *"ecclesia fit religiosorum"* in the genitive sense of possession, so that one must conclude that subsequent to a union effected *pleno iure* the parish and its goods become the *property* of the religious? In the opinion of the writer that is not the correct interpretation of the words *"ecclesia fit religiosa"*.

Canon 1411 describes a benefice as *secular* or *religious* insofar as it pertains to seculars or to religious. A benefice is, therefore, secular or religious insofar as its *title* is to be conferred upon seculars or upon religious. Now, when canon 1425, § 2, states that the parish becomes a religious parish *(paroecia fit religiosa)* it intends merely to state that whereas the *title* to this parish had formerly pertained to a secular cleric, that *title* now pertains to the religious house, precisely because of the union effected *pleno iure* of the parish with the religious house. This fact cannot be denied. In accord with canon 471, subsequent to a union which is effected *pleno iure* the religious house itself becomes the permanently accredited and legally ratified incumbent *in title*, whereas the vicar becomes the transitorily accredited and legally approved incumbent *in administration*. The religious house itself, therefore, acquires the *title* to the parish. However, there seems to be no more reason for concluding that, because the religious house has acquired the *title* to the parish, it has also obtained the dominion over its goods, than there is reason to state that a secular priest acquires dominion or ownership of the parish goods once he has obtained the *title* to the secular parish. And yet, no one will contend that the secular priest acquires the dominion of the goods of the parish with whose *title* he has been vested. Neither, then, should one contend that the religious house obtains the dominion or ownership of the goods *(bona)* of the parish for the simple reason that it has obtained the *title* to the incorporated parish.

The foregoing explanation, therefore, seems to the writer to be the correct interpretation of the words *"paroecia fit religiosa"* in canon 1425, § 2. In accord with this interpretation, it must be admitted that a parish united even *pleno iure* to a religious house retains the status of a *subiectum iuris,* capable of holding and acquiring property in its own name.[31] Indeed, Nebreda states that the conferring of the ownership or dominion of the parish church itself is not to be computed among the effects of an incorporation effected *pleno iure.*[32] That is to say, the union effected *pleno iure* transfers the *title* of the benefice, but the dominion or ownership of its goods is retained by the parish itself. Only the *fructus* of the parish come under the dominion of the religious.

From the foregoing discussion it seems to be clearly indicated that all *property* belongs to the incorporated parish as much after the union as it did before the union. Wherefore, separate administrations are required for the goods pertaining to the parish and for those pertaining to the religious house as such. The goods of the parish and the goods of the religious house cannot, therefore, be considered as forming but one *massa communis* under but one admistration, namely, the administration of the the religious house.[33]

31 "Quando il Codice dice che la *paroecia pleno iure* unita al monastero *fit religiosa,* non intende affatto dire che essa scompare come ente giuridico, e neppure che essa cade *sotto il pieno diritto* 'utendi et abutendi' dei religiosi o regolari. Esso dice soltanto (e lo dichiara espressamente) che dopo e per l'unione la parrocchia ha come rettore abituale una persona morale, *de se perpetua,* quale è il monastero, e quindi deve provedersi in altro modo; ma sussiste tuttavia come soggetto di diritto — che mantiene i suoi beni, e può accrescerli acquistando e disponendo . . ." — Bondini, "Circa il rendiconto del parroco religioso al Vescovo" — *Il Monitore Ecclesiastico,* XXXVIII (1926), 342.

32 "Etenim inter effectus quos gignit incorporatio domui religiosae pleno iure facta, non invenientur ecclesiarum paroecialium, quae incorporantur, dominium aut usus proprie dictus. . . . Quisque videt, et casus aliquos cognoscimus, ecclesiam paroecialem concredi posse pleno iure religiosis exemptis et non exemptis, quin tamen ad ipsos dominium aut usus illius ecclesiae transferatur." — "Quaestiones Selectae de Iure Administrativo Ecclesiastico" — *CpR,* VII (1926), 330.

33 Cf. Goyeneche, "Consultationes" — *CpR,* X (1929), 39-41.

Section 2. The Subject in Whom the Right of Administration Resides

Granted that a separate administration of the property pertaining to the parish is required, it seems but logical to propose the following question. Who, then, is to administer this property?

It is the ruling of the Code that the beneficiary administer the goods pertaining to his benefice.[34] Concerning the administration of the property of a parish incorporated with a religious house *pleno iure,* therefore, there seems to be little difficulty. The religious house itself acquires *title* to the benefice, and thereby becomes its beneficiary. Accordingly, the religious house through its Superior, and not the vicar, becomes the administrator of the property of the parish.[35]

With regard to the administration of the goods of a parish incorporated *ad temporalia tantum* with a religious house, it appears to the writer that the administration pertains to the *sacerdos* mentioned in canon 1425, § 1. In a union which is conceded *ad temporalia tantum* the *iura spiritualia* are not transferred to the religious house; the benefice remains a secular benefice; the *title* to the parish is not transferred to the religious house, but is retained by the secular priest mentioned in canon 1425, § 1; and, finally, according to the writer's contention, the goods of the parish still remain its property even after the union. This *sacerdos* of canon 1425, § 1, therefore, retains the *title* to a parish which is in every sense of the word a true benefice. According to canon 1476, § 1, he, as beneficiary, is charged with the administration of the benefice to which he has title.

It may be objected that the religious house should be the administrator of the property of the parish, since it is to acquire all the *fruits* or *income* of the parish, only a portion thereof being assigned to the *sacerdos* in accord with the ruling of canon 1425, § 1. Such a contention, however, seems to be without a foundation in law, and is in direct contrast to the provision of canon

34 Canon 1476, § 1. Beneficiarius bona ad suum beneficium pertinentia, ut beneficii curator administrare debet, ad normam iuris.

35 Cf. Canon 471; Goyeneche, *art. cit., CpR,* X (1929), 40-42.

1476, § 1. The mere fact that the religious house has an interest in the property does not justify the conclusion that it should, accordingly, be its administrator. There is a parellel case in the Code to illustrate this point. Canon 1429, § 2, permits the local ordinary to impose a pension upon a parochial benefice, in favor of a former pastor or assistant, which grants the right to receive up to one-third of the *income* or *fruits* of the benefice. Now such a pensionary, like the religious house with which a parish has been united *ad temporalia tantum,* has a direct interest in the proper administration of all the parish property. And yet, no right is given the pensionary for this reason to administer the goods of the parish. The administration rather pertains to the actual incumbent of the benefice. It is the writer's contention, therefore, that the goods of a parish united *ad temporalia tantum* with a religious house are to be administered by the *sacerdos* mentioned in canon 1425, § 1, and not by the religious house in the person of the religious Superior.

Section 3. Right of Administration and Vigilance of the Local Ordinary

Finally, it seems opportune to furnish in this last section some notion of other juridical effects consequent upon the doctrine established in the foregoing pages. Only the general principles will be indicated, however, since an examination and commentary upon each of these effects would furnish matter sufficient for another entire dissertation. If it be assumed, then, that in the union of a parish with a religious house, whether conceded *ad temporalia tantum* or effected *pleno iure,* the dominion or ownership of all the parish property (endowment, parish church, real estate, etc.) is not transferred to the religious house, but is rather retained by the parish itself as a distinct *subiectum iuris,* the following conclusions can be established:

I. It pertains to the *religious superior* to accept, to retain, to collect, and to administer offerings *(eleemosynae)* made for the conservation, renovation, or decoration of a parish church, if the church is the *property* of the religious.[36] The mere fact of the

[36] Canon 630, § 4.

union of the parish with the religious house, whether conceded *ad temporalia tantum* or effected *pleno iure,* does not, however, confer the ownership or dominion of the parish property upon the religious house.[37]

II. The retention, collection, and administration of the offerings made for the construction, conservation, renovation, or decoration of a parish church *united* with a religious house, whether *ad temporalia tantum* or *pleno iure,* pertains to the local ordinary, if the parish church is *not* the property of the religious house as such.[38]

III. Local ordinaries have the right of *vigilance* over the administration of all goods given to parishes, missions, or parish churches united *ad temporalia tantum* or *pleno iure* with a religious house, even an exempt religious house, provided that the parish church be the property of the diocese and not the property of the religious as such.[39] This right of vigilance, however, does not comprise within its scope the *fruits* or *income* of a parish united with a religious house, since this income becomes the property of the religious.

IV. Local ordinaries have not the right of vigilance over goods given to a parish united with a religious house, if the parish *church* itself is the *property* of the religious.

V. Local ordinaries have the right of vigilance over the administration of pious foundations established in the parish churches of religious, even of exempt religious, provided that the church itself is the property of the diocese, even though the parish has been incorporated *pleno iure* with the religious house.[40] Again it is stated that the *union* of the parish with the religious

37 Cf. Nebreda, "Quaestiones Selectae de Iure Administrativo Ecclesiastico"—*CpR,* VII (1926), 195.

38 Quocirca cum paroecia unitur pleno iure instituto religioso, paroecia quidem fit religiosa, sed ecclesia potest non esse religiosa: v. gr., episcopus, Sancta Sede interveniente . . . tradit paroecia religiosis; non cedit tamen ecclesiam ipsis, sed manet dioeceseos; tunc enim habetur paroecia religiosa, sed ecclesia non est proprie religiosa."—Nebreda, *art. cit., CpR,* VII (1926), 263; cf. also, canon 630, § 4.

39 Cf. Nebreda, *art. cit., CpR,* VII (1926), 263-264.

40 Cf. Nebreda, *art. cit., CpR,* VII (1926), 329; canons 1545-1549.

house does not of itself transfer the ownership of parish property to the religious house.

VI. Finally, local ordinaries have not the right of vigilance over the administration of pious foundations established in a church of exempt religious, if the church, even though a parish church, is the property of the religious, even if the parish has been united with the religious house simply *ad temporalia tantum.*[41] In such a case the right of vigilance over the administration of such foundations pertains exclusively to the major religious superior.[42]

41 Cf. Nebreda, *art. cit., CpR,* VII (1929) 329.
42 Canon 1550.

CHAPTER V

THE COMPETENCE OF VARIOUS ECCLESIASTICAL SUPERIORS IN THE UNION OF PARISHES

In the preceding chapter consideration was given to the different kinds of union of parishes and their varied juridical effects in accord with the provisions of canons 1419-1420. With these notions well in mind, one can now proceed to determine the ecclesiastical superiors competent in effecting the union of parishes, and the types of union they can effect in accord with their established competence.

As stated repeatedly in this work, any form of the union of parishes whatsoever is considered in law as odious. The more odious the form of union, the more reluctant has the Holy See been to grant to inferior legislators the power to effect such unions. Accordingly, the Code of Canon Law has seen fit to reserve expressly to the exclusive competence of the Holy See the more odious forms of union of parishes. In effecting certain other less odious forms of union, however, the Holy See shares its competence with local ordinaries.

The purpose of this chapter, therefore, will be to determine, in different articles: 1) the types of union reserved in law to the exclusive competence of the Holy See; 2) the specification of those who are to be understood as local ordinaries with regard to the union of parishes; 3) the types of union within the competence of local ordinaries; and, finally, 4) the types of union expressly forbidden to local ordinaries.

Article 1. The Types of the Union of Parishes Reserved to the Exclusive Competence of the Holy See

Canon 1422. Unio extinctiva beneficiorum . . . unio aeque aut minus principalis beneficii religiosi cum saeculari et contra . . . uni Sedi Apostolicae reservantur.

The Code in canon 1422 reserves to the exclusive competence of the Holy See the extinctive union of benefices, and therefore also the extinctive union of parishes. The notion of an extinctive union is to be found in canon 1419, 1°, and has already been discussed in detail.[1]

The power of local ordinaries to effect the union of parishes will be developed more fully in a subsequent article.[2] It will, therefore, be sufficient to state at this point that up until the Code extinctive unions were within the scope of competence of local ordinaries. Originally the power of bishops to unite benefices was rather extensive.[3] As time went on, however, restrictions were placed upon this power; but nowhere in pre-Code legislation can there be found any provision which excluded the effecting of extinctive unions from the competence of local ordinaries. Accordingly, one must conclude that the provision of the Code which reserves all extinctive unions to the exclusive competence of the Holy See constitutes a change in the law.

The second form of union reserved by canon 1422 to the Holy See is that wherein a secular benefice is either co-ordinatively or subordinatively united with a religious benefice or vice versa. Since the first part of canon 1422 reserves to the Holy See all forms of extinctive union, among which must be enumerated the extinctive union of a secular and a religious parish, and since the later section of the same canon likewise reserves to the Holy See a co-ordinative or a subordinative union of a secular and a religious parish, one must conclude that any and all forms of the union of these two types of parishes are reserved to the Holy See.

Benefices are secular or religious according as their title pertains exclusively to the secular or to the religious clergy.[4] As shall be seen presently, it is within the competence of local ordinaries to unite parishes by way of a co-ordinative or a subordinative union, whether secular or non-exempt religious in character, provided only that a secular parish be united to a secular parish, and a religious to a religious.[5] Canon 1422, however, excludes

1 *Supra*, p. 52.

2 *Infra*, p. 91.

3 Cf. c. 8, X, *de excessibus praelatorum*, V, 31.

4 Canon 1411, 2°.

5 Canon 1423, § 1. Ordinarii locorum . . . possunt . . . aeque aut minus principaliter unire *quaslibet* paroeciales ecclesias . . .

from the competence of local ordinaries the indiscriminate union of a secular with a religious benefice. Such a union, if executed, must be performed by the Holy See.

The Code in employing the words *"uni" Sedi Apostolicae* does so with definite design. Because of the insertion of the word *"uni"*, the competence of the Holy See in the matter of uniting a secular parish with a religious parish, as well as in all extinctive unions, is rendered exclusive; and such union effected by any other superior contrary to the provision of the canon must thereby be considered as invalid. Canon 11 states that only those laws are to be considered as invalidating in which it is expressly or equivalently stated that the act is null.[6] It would appear that the use of the word *"uni"* constitutes an instance wherein it is equivalently stated that any act contrary to the provision of canon 1422 is invalid.[7]

Article 2. Competence of Local Ordinaries

Canon 1423, § 1. Ordinarii locorum, non autem Vicarius Capitularis, nec Vicarius Generalis sine mandato speciali . . . possunt . . . aeque aut minus principaliter unire quaslibet paroeciales ecclesias. . .

Section 1. Competence of Local Ordinaries in the Old Law

In the old law, as in the law of the Code, the local ordinary was empowered to effect the union of benefices subject to his jurisdiction. Explicit confirmation of this right is to be found in a famous Decretal of Celestine III written to a certain Bishop Faustinus some time between 1191-1198.[8] Since this Decretal is the only one to be found as touching upon the point in question, it has been considered advisable to quote the pertinent portion of the Decretal in its entirety:

> Sicut unire episcopatus atque potestati subiicere alienae, ad summum Pontificem pertinere dignoscitur, ita *episcopi est*

6 Canon 11. Irritantes . . . eae tantum leges habendae sunt, quibus . . . actum esse nullum . . . expresse vel aequivalenter statuitur.

7 Blat, *Commentarium*, III, n. 321.

8 This Decretal has been attributed by some to Clement III (1187-1191). Cf. Jaffé, *Regesta Pontificum Romanorum*, n. 17627.

> ecclesiarum suae dioecesis unio et subiectio earundem. Cum itaque Prior Grandensis monasterium suum, quod est in tua dioecesi, et de tuo debet ordinari consensu, Monasterio de Accato (tuo assensu minime requisito) subiiceret sive unierit: quod fecit te inconsulto, tibi liceat auctoritate nostra (sicut iustum fuerit) infirmare, non obstante assensu vel confirmatione quam Metropolitanus interposuisse proponitur, cum in dioecesi sui suffraganei absque ipsius assensu non debeat aliquid contra constitutiones canonicas attentare, Nos quoque id decernimus irritandum.[9]

In this Decretal Celestine III (1191-1198) clearly vindicated the right of the bishop, and of the bishop alone, to unite the benefices within his diocese. Wherefore, no other inferior prelate could, without the consent of the bishop, unite or subject his benefice to that of another. Nor was the consent of the Metropolitan of any avail if the benefices concerned in the union were to be found not within his diocese but merely within his province. The words of the Decretal itself clearly establish this fact. Indeed, according to Clement V, in the Council of Vienne (1311-1312), so extensive and so exclusive was this power of the bishop to unite benefices within his diocese that he could do so without the consent of the rector of the church concerned in the union.[10]

There can be no doubt, therefore, that the competence of the bishop in uniting parishes subject to his jurisdiction had already been well established under Decretal law. Indeed, this power of the bishop was almost all-embracing. With the passing of the years this competence of the bishop was restricted somewhat; it was, however, never totally denied him. The Council of Trent (1545-1563), while restricting the power, nonetheless recognized and confirmed this competence of bishops.[11]

9 C. 8, X, *de excessibus praelatorum et subditorum*, V, 31.

10 "Si una ecclesia alteri ecclesiae seu dignitati alicui vel praebendae *per episcopum* uniatur, aut religioso loco donetur; ex eo, quod rector ipsius ad hoc vocatus, vel si vacabat, si defensor ei super hoc datus non exstitit, nequaquam id poterit impugnari." — c. 2, *de rebus ecclesiae non alienandis*, III, 4, in Clem.

11 "Ut etiam Ecclesiarum status . . . ex dignitate conservetur, possint Episcopi, etiam tamquam Apostolicae Sedis delegati, iuxta formam iuris,

Section 2. Competence of Local Ordinaries in the Code of Canon Law

The competence of the local ordinary to unite parishes as now established in the Code of Canon Law is not so extensive as was that same power in Decretal law and in the enactments of the Council of Trent. The Code in canons 1423, § 2, and 1424 has restricted the power which ordinaries originally enjoyed. It has, however, been deemed advisable to assign a separate article to the investigation of these restrictions. The present section, therefore, will concern itself not with the unions which the local ordinary can or cannot effect according to present-day legislation, but rather with a consideration of those who are empowered to effect unions under the law of the Code.

Local ordinaries, but not the vicar capitular, nor the vicar general without a special mandate, may because of the needs or the great and evident utility of the Church effect a co-ordinative or also subordinative union of parishes among themselves or with a benefice which has not attached to it the care of souls, provided that in the subordinative union the benefice which has not attached to it the care of souls be made accessory to the parochial benefice.[12]

By *ordinaries* are to be understood in law, unless explicit exception be made in individual instances, besides the Roman Pontiff, the following: within their respective territories the residential bishop, the abbot and prelate *nullius* (and their vicars general), the administrator, the vicar and the prefect apostolic. Furthermore, those persons are ordinaries who, in case of the vacancy of the offices here listed, succeed to the office during its vacancy by the provisions of the law or of approved constitutions. In exempt clerical institutions the major superiors are ordinaries over their subjects.[13] By the term *local ordinaries* are

sine tamen praeiudicio obtinentium, facere uniones perpetuas quarumcumque Ecclesiarum parochialium . . ." — Conc. Trident., sess. XXI, *de ref.*, c. 5.

12 Canon 1423, § 1.

13 Canon 198, § 1.

to be understood all persons enumerated in canon 198, § 1, with the exception of major religious superiors.[14]

According to the provision of canon 198, §§ 1, 2, therefore, the following is a complete list of all those who are, or can be in determined circumstances, local ordinaries: the Roman Pontiff,[15] the residential bishop,[16] abbots or prelates *nullius*,[17] their vicars general,[18] the Apostolic administrator,[19] the vicar apostolic and the prefect apostolic,[20] the cathedral chapter,[21] the diocesan consultors,[22] the vicar capitular (diocesan administrator),[23] the pro-vicar and the pro-prefect,[24] the one deputed in turn by these in the event of their demise or some other hindrance,[25] the senior priest,[26] and the one designated by the bishop in the event of the latter's exile, relegation, or total disability.[27]

Canon 1423, § 1, states in general that local ordinaries, except the vicar capitular and also the vicar general who has no special mandate, are competent to effect certain forms of the union of parishes. It would appear, however, that the Code in excepting the competence of the vicar capitular thereby excludes the competence of certain other local ordinaries enumerated either directly or indirectly in canon 198, §§ 1-2, whose jurisdiction is identical with that of the vicar capitular. Wherefore, it will be necessary to examine the competence of each of the local ordinaries enumerated above to determine which are capable of effecting the union of parishes and which are excluded in law from such a course of action.

14 Canon 198, § 2.
15 Canon 218, § 1.
16 Canons 329, § 1; 334, § 1.
17 Canons 319, § 1; 323, § 1.
18 Canons 366, § 1; 368, § 1; 429, § 1.
19 Canons 312; 315, §§ 1, 2.
20 Canons 293, § 1; 294, § 1.
21 Canons 431, § 1; 435, § 1; 327, § 1.
22 Canons 423, 427.
23 Canons 429, § 3; 432, §§ 1-4; 435, § 1.
24 Canon 309, § 2.
25 Canon 309, § 3.
26 Canon 309, § 4.
27 Canon 429, §§ 1-2.

a. *The Roman Pontiff.* It would seem almost superfluous to state that the Roman Pontiff is competent to effect any type of the union of parishes whatsoever; for as the Supreme Head of the Church every manner of jurisdictional activity is admittedly within his power.[28] Accordingly, there need be no delay for the sake of proving this point.

b. *The Residential Bishop.* The residential bishop is most certainly to be included under the term *ordinarii locorum* as employed in canon 1423, § 1, for canon 198, § 1, states that he is to be considered as a local ordinary unless he be expressly excepted. Canon 1423, § 1, however, mentions no exception in his regard. So long, therefore, as he legitimately retains possession of his office, the residential bishop is competent to effect the unions of parishes as proposed in canon 1423, § 1. Should he, however, canonically renounce his office or be canonically deprived thereof, as in all other matters of jurisdiction, so, too, his power to unite parishes would cease at the moment the renunciation or deprivation goes into effect.[29]

In the event that a residential bishop is *transferred* from one see to another, however, his power to unite parishes ceases from the moment the notification of his transfer is intimated to him. From the time this intimation is made until the bishop assumes canonical possession of his new see, he obtains in his former diocese the powers of a vicar capitular.[30] The vicar capitular is, however, expressly forbidden in canon 1423, § 1, to effect the union of parishes.[31]

The rights of a coadjutor bishop with regard to the union of parishes differ according to the extent of his jurisdiction. The rights of a coadjutor given to the person of a bishop are to be sought primarily in the apostolic letters of appointment.[32] Unless, however, it is otherwise stated in these letters, the coadjutor

28 Pirhing, *Jus Canonicum,* lib. III, tit. V, n. 204; Schmalzgrueber, lib. III, tit. V, n. 170; Reiffenstuel, lib. III, tit. XII, n. 52.

29 Canons 183, § 1; 190, § 1; 192, §§ 1-3; 430, § 1.

30 Canon 430, § 3, 1°.

31 Cf. Augustine, *The Canonical and Civil Status of Catholic Parishes in the United States,* pp. 59-60.

32 Canon 351, § 1.

given to the person of a bishop who is entirely incapacitated has by law all the rights and duties of a residential bishop.[33] Such a coadjutor can, accordingly, effect those unions of parishes which are permitted by law to a residential bishop. In doing so he acts in virtue of his ordinary power.[34]

On the other hand, if the bishop of the see to whom he is assigned is not entirely incapacitated, the coadjutor has power to effect the union of parishes only if such power is granted him by his letters of appointment or by the bishop of the diocese.[35] In such a case the coadjutor would act in virtue of delegated jurisdiction.[36] In a similar manner, a coadjutor given not to the person of a bishop but to the see itself can effect the union of parishes only when such competence is delegated to him.[37]

c. *Abbots and Prelates Nullius.* Abbots and prelates *nullius* have in the matter of the union of parishes the same ordinary competence as that of a residential bishop, for they, too, are included as local ordinaries under canon 198, § 1, and no exception in their regard is to be found in canon 1423, § 1.[38] This ordinary power, however, is granted to abbots or prelates *nullius* only if their abbacy or prelacy *nullius* consists of at least three parishes, for an abbacy or prelacy *nullius* which does not consist of at least three parishes is ruled by special laws, and to such does not apply what the canons state concerning abbacies and prelacies *nullius*.[39] Moreover, there would scarcely be need to establish the competence of abbots or prelates *nullius* if the abbacy or prelacy consisted of but one, or at the most, two parishes, for a union of the parishes would scarcely be desirable.

33 Canon 351, § 2.

34 Canon 197, § 1.

35 Canon 351, §§ 1-2.

36 Canon 197, § 1; 199, § 1.

37 Canon 352. Coadjutor sedi datus potest in territorio ea quae sunt ordinis episcopalis exercere, excepta sacra ordinatione; *aliis in rebus* tantum potest quantum eidem a Sancta Sede vel ab Episcopo fuerit commissum.

38 Canon 323, § 1. Abbas vel Prelatus *nullius* easdem potestates ordinarias easdemque obligationes cum iisdem sanctionibus habet, quae competunt episcopis residentialibus in propria dioecesi.

39 Canon 319, § 2.

However, should such a union actually become imperative, the competency of the abbot or prelate *nullius* in such a case must be derived from special law, not from the law of the Code as established in canon 1423, § 1.

d. *The Vicar General.* The vicar general has by virtue of his office jurisdiction over the entire diocese in spiritual and temporal matters to the extent of the bishop's ordinary jurisdiction, except in those affairs which the bishop has reserved to himself, or which by law postulate a special mandate from the bishop.[40] Canon 1423, § 1, affords an instance wherein the vicar general cannot act validly without a special mandate from the bishop. He cannot, therefore, according to the law of the Code, validly effect a union of parishes unless he have this special mandate. This provision of the Code is in full conformity with the old law.[41]

e. *The Apostolic Administrator.* The rights, duties, and privileges of the apostolic administrator are to be adjudged from his letter of appointment, or if the letter does not expressly state otherwise, according to the rules enacted in canons 315-318.[42] The letter of appointment sometimes contains a mere announcement to the effect that a certain person has been designated by the Holy See as apostolic administrator. At other times, however, it contains a detailed enumeration of the various rights, duties, and privileges of the person named in this capacity. Of these rights, duties, and privileges, some may be in accord with the common law; others may be rights, duties and privileges over and beyond the common law; still others, finally, may be rights, duties, and privileges which connote for the apostolic administrator a restriction or limitation relative to what he would normally enjoy according to the law of the Code. Wherefore, it is of the utmost importance and a matter for prime consideration that the letter of appointment be examined first to

40 Canon 368, § 1.

41 Garcia, *De Beneficiis,* pars XII, cap. II, n. 69; Schmalzgrueber, lib. III, tit. V, n. 180; Reiffenstuel, lib. III, tit. XII, n. 65.

42 Canon 314.

determine just what rights, duties and privileges have actually been attributed to this office.[43]

In the event that the letter of appointment contains no specification of rights, duties, and privileges, these must be determined from the common law.[44] According to the law of the Code, an apostolic administrator whose appointment is *perpetual* enjoys the same rights and honors, and is bound by the same obligations, as the residential bishop.[45] Such an administrator can, therefore, like a residential bishop, effect the unions of parishes as mentioned in canon 1423, § 1.[46] A *temporary* apostolic administrator, on the other hand, has the same rights and duties as the vicar capitular.[47] Canon 1423, § 1, however, expressly excludes the vicar capitular from the local ordinaries empowered under its provision to effect the union of parishes. Wherefore, like the vicar capitular, so, too, a *temporary* apostolic administrator cannot effect validly the union of parishes.

f. *The Cathedral Chapter, Sede Vacante.* The commentators upon the old law seem to have entertained some doubt as to the power of the cathedral chapter to unite parishes in the vacancy of the see. This doubt arose because of the lack of capacity on the part of the cathedral chapter to *confer* a benefice under such circumstances. It was, however, contended that no union could be made apart from the simultaneous appointment of a beneficiary. Hence, the conclusion seems to have been that the cathedral chapter was incapable of *uniting* parishes.

This conclusion was, however, attacked for various reasons. In the first place, it was contended that the bishop could not *confer* benefices if their conferment was the right of subordinate prelates or electors; yet he could with their consent *unite* them.

43 For a more detailed treatment of this subject, cf. McDonough, *Apostolic Administrators,* The Catholic University of America Canon Law Studies, n. 139 (Washington, D. C.: The Catholic University of America Press, 1941), pp. 83-91.

44 Canon 315, 316.

45 Canon 315, § 1.

46 McDonough, *Apostolic Administrators,* p. 102, n. 11.

47 Canon 315, § 2, 1°.

Secondly, a benefice not as yet vacant could not validly be *conferred;* it was subject, however, to the possibility of being *united* with some other benefice. Thirdly, the right to *confer* and the right to *unite* emanate from entirely different sources. The conferring of a benefice is an act of liberality, coming from a free act of the will. The uniting of a benefice, on the other hand, is not a matter of choice but of necessity if the canonical causes and solemnities are present. Wherefore, it was generally conceded by authors that the cathedral chapter in the vacancy of the see was empowered to unite parishes.[48]

Canon 1423, § 1, explicitly excludes from the category of local ordinaries only the vicar capitular and the vicar general who has no special mandate. Therefore, according to canon 198, § 1, which states that, unless they are expressly excluded, there are to be understood in law as local ordinaries those persons who in the case of a vacancy of the office succeed thereto by the provisions of the law or of approved custom, it can be argued that the cathedral chapter still enjoys under the law of the Code the right to unite parishes.

One must note, however, that in the Code a power may be granted or denied expressly *(expresse)* and yet implicitly *(implicite)*. Jurisdiction can be granted interpretatively, tacitly, or expressly.[49] Express jurisdiction, however, can be either *explicit* or *implicit*. Express jurisdiction is said to be granted or denied *explicitly* when the very words of the law state so. Express jurisdiction, on the other hand, is granted or denied *implicitly* when, without the aid of a specific statement, the purport and force of such a grant or denial is contained in what has been stated either explicitly or with equivalent effect.[50]

48 Garcia, *De Beneficiis,* pars XII, cap. II, n. 67; Pirhing, *Jus Canonicum,* lib. III, tit. V, n. 207; Schmalzgrueber, lib. III, tit. V, n. 175; Reiffenstuel, lib. III, tit. XII, n. 57.

49 Gasparri, *De Matrimonio* (ed. nova, 2 vols., Romae: Typis Polyglottis Vaticanis, 1932), II, n. 954.

50 Cf. Reilly, *The General Norms of Dispensation,* The Catholic University of America Canon Law Studies, n. 119 (Washington, D. C.: The Catholic University of America Press, 1939), pp. 66, 68.

It is the contention of the writer that the Code in canon 1423, § 1, by explicitly excluding the vicar capitular, *expressly* though *implicitly* excludes also the cathedral chapter. Moreover, it is easily understandable why the legislator chose to employ the term "vicar capitular" rather than the term "cathedral chapter" in canon 1423, § 1. Although the office both of the vicar capitular and of the cathedral chapter is of a temporary nature during the vacancy of the see, still the office of the vicar capitular is more stable and more enduring than that of the cathedral chapter. According to law, the cathedral chapter upon the vacancy of the see governs the diocese, but must within a period of eight days following the notification of the vacancy constitute a vicar capitular.[51]

Now, it is possible that circumstances necessitating the union of parishes could arise in such a short time. It is more likely, however, that they could arise during the longer term of government exercised by the vicar capitular. And yet, the Code in canon 1423, § 1, denies to the vicar capitular the power to effect the union of parishes. Is it reasonable, then, to conclude that this power is given to the cathedral chapter but denied to the vicar capitular?

The writer's contention is further strengthened by a consideration of the identity that exists between the jurisdiction of the cathedral chapter and that of the vicar capitular. The jurisdiction of the cathedral chapter is, after a canonical election, passed on to the vicar capitular, who thenceforth governs the diocese in the name of the chapter. Consequently, the number of persons participating in the power, but not the nature of the power itself, is changed. In the vacancy of the see both the vicar capitular and the chapter are governed by the same principle: *sede vacante, nihil innovetur.*[52] Granted, therefore, that according to law the scope of jurisdiction of the cathedral chapter and that of the vicar capitular is the same, whatever power is granted the one is likewise granted the other and vice versa. The vicar capitular, however, is by law incapable of effecting the union of

51 Canon 432, § 1.

52 Canon 436.

parishes. The cathedral chapter accordingly shares in this lack of jurisdiction.

g. *The Diocesan Consultors.* The body of diocesan consultors takes the place of the cathedral chapter as the council of the bishop; wherefore, whatever part in the government of the diocese the canons attribute to the cathedral chapter during the reign of the bishop, during the time the exercise of his jurisdiction is impeded, or during the vacancy of the see, is also assigned to the body of diocesan consultors.[53] Consequently, the diocesan consultors, like the cathedral chapter, seem to be expressly though implicitly excluded by canon 1423, § 1, from being empowered to effect the union of parishes.

h. *The Vicar Capitular or Administrator.* Commentators on the old law held that the vicar capitular, like the cathedral chapter, was capable of effecting the union of parishes.[54] There exists today even under the law of the Code a grave doubt as to the competence of the vicar capitular in effecting the *division* of parishes.[55] Such a doubt cannot be entertained, however, with reference to the *union* of parishes. The Code in canon 1423, § 1, is explicit in denying to the vicar capitular the power to unite parishes.[56]

Administrators are employed for the government of a vacant diocese in those countries in which cathedral chapters are nonexistent. Whatever power is attributed in the Code to the cathedral chapter concerning the government of a vacant diocese is likewise to be understood as applying to the diocesan consultors.[57] As the cathedral chapter, in accord with canon 432, § 1, is obligated to elect a vicar capitular within eight days, so, too, the diocesan consultors within the same length of time must elect an administrator, unless the Holy See has provided otherwise.

53 Canon 427.

54 Cf. Craisson (+1881), *Manuale Totius Juris Canonici* (ed. 6., 4 vols., Patavii, 1880), I, n. 357.

55 Connolly, *The Canonical Erection of Parishes,* pp. 48-50.

56 Canon 1423, § 1. Ordinarii locorum, non autem Vicarius Capitularis . . . possunt . . . aeque aut minus principaliter unire quaslibet paroeciales ecclesias . . .

57 Canon 427.

The office of this administrator is identical with that of the vicar capitular. Canon 1423, § 1, however, as has been pointed out, denies competence to the vicar capitular in the union of parishes. The conclusion must necessarily follow, therefore, that the administrator of a vacant diocese shares in law the condition of a vicar capitular and is, accordingly, incapable of validly effecting the union of parishes by reason of his ordinary power in ruling the diocese.

i. *The Prefect or Vicar Apostolic.* To determine the competence of prefects or vicars apostolic with reference to the union of parishes is, strictly considered, not within the confines of this dissertation. The writer is treating of the canonical norms governing the union of *parishes.* Parishes, however, are defined by the Code as the subordinate parts of a canonical diocese.[58] Prefects and vicars apostolic, on the other hand, govern prefectures or vicariates whose subordinate parts come in law under the title of *quasi-parishes.*[59] Because of the similarity of parishes and quasi-parishes, however, the matter merits some consideration.

In an earlier part of this work the writer adhered to the opinion of Maroto that parishes and quasi-parishes, so far as their legal nature and constituent parts are concerned, are identically the same. The diversity of names is derived solely from their relationship to the hierarchical unit of which they are part.[60] Moreover, quasi-pastors are by law equivalent to pastors.[61] Exceptions to this principle, however, are to be found in the Code, and have already been mentioned in the foregoing pages.[62]

Vicars and prefects apostolic enjoy in their respective territories the same rights and faculties as residential bishops, unless the Holy See has made some restriction in a particular case.[63] Wherefore, they have not only the right but also the obligation

58 Canon 216 § 3.

59 Canon 216, § 3.

60 *Supra,* p. 11; Connolly, *The Canonical Erection of Parishes,* p. 6.

61 Canon 451, § 2, 1°.

62 *Supra,* p. 11, footnote 30.

63 Canon 294, § 1.

to *erect* quasi-parishes wherever this can be done conveniently.[64] The Sacred Congregation of the Propagation of the Faith has supplemented the law of the Code by instructing local ordinaries as to the manner and the advisability of erecting quasi-parishes.[65]

But are vicars and prefects apostolic empowered under canon 1423, § 1, to effect the *union* of quasi-parishes? Certainly they can be included under the term *Ordinarii locorum* of this canon, for canon 198, § 1, states that they are to be considered as such unless they are expressly excepted. No exception in their regard is to be found, however, in canon 1423, § 1. The answer to the question, therefore, depends upon the interpretation given the words *paroeciales ecclesias* in canon 1423, § 1. If these words be interpreted strictly, then they seem to exclude quasi-parishes. But if, on the other hand, in view of the identical legal nature of parishes and quasi-parishes, a wider interpretation is given them, then quasi-parishes can be included under the legislation of canon 1423, § 1, and vicars and prefects apostolic can effect the union of quasi-parishes. The writer inclines towards this latter opinion.

But even if a strict interpretation of the words *paroeciales ecclesias* in canon 1423, § 1, be insisted upon, still another argument can be adduced to support the writer's opinion. There is no denying that the circumstances which necessitate or counsel the union of parishes can arise just as easily, if not more easily, in a prefecture or a vicariate as they can in an established diocese. Granting, therefore, that vicars and prefects are not empowered under the strict letter of the law of canon 1423, § 1, to effect unions, where in the entire Code shall legislation be found to meet such contingencies should they at any time arise in the vicariate or prefecture?

At the very least one would be compelled to admit a *lacuna* in the law of the Code. In the event, however, that no express provision is to be found concerning some matter either in the

64 Canon 216, §2; Winslow, *Vicars and Prefects Apostolic,* The Catholic University of America Canon Law Studies, n. 24 (Washington, D. C.: The Catholic University of America, 1924), pp. 57-60; Connolly, *The Canonical Erection of Parishes,* p. 45.

65 S. C. Prop. Fide, instr., 25 iul. 1929, n. 1, 4 — *AAS,* XII (1920), 331.

general or in the particular law, a norm of action is then to be taken from laws given in similar cases.[66] So far as the writer has been able to ascertain, no particular law has been issued by the Holy See which would afford a solution to the case in question. Granting, therefore, that there is neither a general nor a particular law in the case, one can justly employ canon 20 along with canon 1423, § 1, to conclunde that vicars and prefects apostolic are competent in effecting the union of quasi-parishes.

j. *Other Temporary Ordinaries.* Canon 309, §§ 2-4, makes provision for the government of the prefecture or vicariate apostolic in the event of the demise of the prefect or vicar apostolic. In such a case, the pro-vicar or pro-prefect, the one deputed in turn by these in the event of their demise or some other hindrance, or the senior priest succeeds in turn to the office of the vicar or prefect apostolic. It seems, however, that none of these is competent to effect a union of the quasi-parishes of the prefecture or vicariate apostolic, since their term in office is strictly temporary or provisional, and in this respect like to that of the cathedral chapter or the vicar capitular in the government of a vacant or quasi-vacant diocese. The vicar capitular and the cathedral chapter, however, as has already been demonstrated, lack the necessary competence in this matter.

In like manner the vicar general or the one designated by the bishop in accord with the provision of canon 429, §§ 1-2, in the event of the latter's exile, relegation, etc., seems to be equally incompetent in the matter of uniting parishes. Canon 1423, § 1, expressly excludes the vicar general who has not a special mandate, yet who enjoys in the diocese the exercise of ordinary jurisdiction. There seems to be no valid reason for denying competence to him, and yet for according it to the cleric deputed by the bishop who governs with mere delegated power.

66 Canon 20. Si certa de re desit expressum praescriptum legis sive generalis sive particularis, norma sumenda est . . . a legibus latis in similibus . . .

ARTICLE 3. THE TYPES OF UNION PERMITTED TO LOCAL ORDINARIES

Canon 1423, § 1. Ordinarii locorum, non autem Vicarius Capitularis, nec Vicarius Generalis sine mandato speciali, possunt, ob Ecclesiae necessitatem vel magnam et evidentem utilitatem, aeque aut minus principaliter unire quaslibet paroeciales ecclesias inter se aut cum beneficio non curato, ita tamen ut altero in casu, si unio fiat minus principalis, beneficium non curatum sit accessorium.

Canon 1423, § 2. . . . sed possunt eam [paroeciam] cum ecclesia cathedrali aut collegiali, quae in territorio paroeciae sita sit, ita unire ut reditus paroeciae cedant in commodum ipsius ecclesiae, relicta parocho vel vicario congrua portione.

Having determined in the preceding article those who are to be understood as local ordinaries with reference to the union of parishes, one can now proceed to determine the types of unions which they can effect in virtue of the provisions of canon 1423, §§ 1, 2. Local ordinaries, but not the vicar capitular, nor the vicar general who has not a special mandate, may, because of the needs or the great and evident utility of the Church, effect a co-ordinative or also a subordinative union of parishes among themselves or with a benefice to which is not attached the care of souls, provided that in the subordinative union the benefice which is not vested with the care of souls be made accessory to the parish.[67]

There is to be found in canon 1423, § 1, an assignment of the canonical causes required for the validity of any union of parishes. The presence and discernment thereof is, indeed, of the greatest importance, for any union of parishes executed without such a canonical cause is invalid.[68] Because of the importance of this point, therefore, but especially because of the desire to treat of this subject in its proper place, it has been deemed ad-

67 Canon 1423, § 1.

68 Canon 1428, § 2.

visable to consign the matter of the necessary canonical causes to the following chapter, which will consider the general requisites for any form of the union of parishes.[69]

The canon states that local ordinaries can *(possunt)* unite parishes according to the manner prescribed therein. The word *"possunt"* of itself implies simply that the power to effect the union of parishes is granted to local ordinaries. But is this to be understood as a power which they may or may not employ according to their desire in the matter? Or, other than the *right*, must one understand also the corresponding *obligation* to effect such unions?

Schmalzgrueber maintained that the union of benefices was a matter of necessity, and not simply of discretional choice.[70] That is to say, once the conditions warranting a union were ascertained as being actually present, the union had of necessity to be accomplished. The very concept of the union of parishes seems to lend credence to this opinion. It has been stated repeatedly that the power to bring about such unions is granted not in favor of any one individual, but in view of the greater good of the Church as a whole. Should, then, the condition of one or more benefices necessitate the intervention of a union of benefices, the ordinary, who is entrusted with fostering the welfare of that part of the Church committed to his care, must take whatever steps are required in that direction. And if the union of the benefices affords the only solution for the case, then he is bound to effect such a union. It seems to the writer, therefore, that a wider interpretation is to be given to the word *"possunt"* than that which is afforded by its etymological signification. When conditions so warrant, local ordinaries not only can *(possunt)*, but must *(debent)*, effect the union of parishes.

In executing the union of parishes local ordinaries are limited by the words of canon 1423, § 1, to the sphere of *co-ordinative* and *subordinative* unions. *Extinctive* unions are forbidden to them both by the silence of the law in canon 1423, § 1, and espe-

69 *Infra,* p. 128.

70 "Non idem jus est de conferendo et uniendo; nam conferre est voluntatis et liberalitatis; at unire est necessitatis . . ." — lib. III, tit. V, n. 175.

cially by the explicit prohibition of canon 1422. Circumstances in the individual case will generally indicate to the ordinary which of the two permissible forms constitutes the happier choice. Thus, if it is found necessary to unite parishes simply because of a temporary shortage of suitable pastors, the revenues of both benefices being sufficient for their needs, the co-ordinative form of union seems to be the more advisable, since it requires a separate administration of the revenues of both benefices. But if, on the other hand, the lack of revenue of one or more parishes affords the principal reason for uniting them to some other parish, then a subordinative union would certainly seem to be more desirable, in order that the goods of one might lawfully be used in support of the needs of the other. Such a procedure, however, would not be possible were the parishes united by way of a co-ordinative union. The various juridical effects of each of these forms of union must be pondered well, therefore, before the type of union is decided upon.[71]

Proceeding further in its legislation the Code states that local ordinaries are empowered to effect the union of *any kind* of parishes *(quaslibet paroeciales ecclesias).* Is the word *"quaslibet"*, then, to be interpreted as enabling local ordinaries to unite religious parishes among themselves as well as secular? Pistocchi is of the opinion that such is to be the interpretation given to the word *"quaslibet."*[72] Blat[73] and Vermeersch-Creusen maintain a similar opinion.[74] Coronata, on the contrary, contends that this power of local ordinaries does not extend itself to religious parishes.[75] Indeed, he cites Vermeersch-Creusen as sharing this

71 These effects have already been discussed in detail, cf. *supra*, pp. 64-70.

72 "Vis canonis, ut supra notavimus, est sita in facultate noviter facta Ordinariis uniendi paroeciales ecclesias, etiam religiosorum, contra praescriptum cap. 13, *de ref.*, Conc. Trident., sess. XXIV, superius citatum." — *De Re Beneficiali*, p. 88.

73 *Commentarium*, III, pars altera, n. 322.

74 *Epitome*, II, n. 754.

75 "Inter casus exclusos adnumerandi etiam sunt casus in cc. 1422 et 1424 relati, ideo nequit Ordinarius loci ordinaria potestate unire paroecias religiosorum." — *Institutiones Iuris Canonici*, II, n. 980, p. 372, footnote, 4.

opinion.[76] The express words to the contrary employed by Vermeersch-Creusen, however, show this citation to be erroneous.[77]

The writer is inclined to agree with those who state that because of the employment of the words *"quaslibet" paroeciales ecclesias* in canon 1423, § 1, local ordinaries must be considered as empowered to unite religious parishes among themselves as well as secular. Local ordinaries can, therefore, under the provision of canon 1423, § 1, unite parishes *inter se* whether they be secular or non-exempt religious parishes. In doing so, however, they must see to it that secular parishes are united with secular parishes and religious with religious, for canon 1422 states expressly that the union of a secular with a religious benefice or vice versa is reserved to the Apostolic See. Canon 1423, § 1, contains no exception to this ruling. The provision of canon 1422 must, therefore, be observed.

Canon 1423, § 1, attributes to local ordinaries the power not only of uniting parishes among themselves, but also the competence necessary for uniting a parish with a benefice to which the care of souls is not annexed. Prior to the Code benefices with and without the annexed care of souls *(curata et non-curata)* did not form a separate classification of benefices. At that time a benefice with the care of souls was known as a *beneficium duplex;* a benefice without the care of souls, on the contrary, was classified as a *beneficium simplex.*[78] Now, the Council of Trent had forbidden the union of parishes with *simple* benefices.[79] Since, however, benefices without the care of souls were at that time considered as simple benefices, it follows that the Council of Trent had forbidden the union of parishes with benefices to which the care of souls was not annexed. The provision of canon 1423, § 1,

76 *Institutiones Iuris Canonici, loc. cit.*

77 "Sola tamen permittitur unio aeque principalis vel minus principalis, quacum beneficia remanent; necesse quoque est ut fiat inter beneficia omnia saecularia vel omnia religiosa (ex c. 1422) . . ." — *Epitome,* II, n. 754, 2.

78 Schmalzgrueber, lib. III, tit. V, nn. 30-31; Pistocchi, *De Re Beneficiali,* pp. 28-29; Cocchi, *Commentarium,* III, n. 83.

79 "In unionibus vero quibuslibet . . . Ecclesiae parochiales . . . aliis beneficiis simplicibus . . . non uniantur . . ." — Conc. Trident., sess. XXIV, *de ref.,* c. 13.

permitting such a union must, therefore, be considered as a change in the law.[80]

It has already been pointed out in the treatment of the juridical effects of the various types of union that in a subordinative union the benefice which is united with another becomes its accessory, and follows the nature of the principal benefice.[81] The legislator has been unwilling that a parish should become accessory to a benefice to which the care of souls is not annexed. Hence, though the union of a parish with a benefice unaccredited with the care of souls is permitted by the Code, it must be executed in such a fashion that the benefice which makes no demands for the care of souls be made accessory to the parish, and not vice versa.

Still another form in effecting the union of parishes is within the competence of local ordinaries. According to the last clause of canon 1423, § 2, local ordinaries can unite a parish with the cathedral, or with a collegiate church which is situated within the territorial limits of the parish, a suitable portion of the income therefrom having been assigned to its pastor or vicar. This paragraph of canon 1423 deals with what are known in law as the forms of the *incorporation* of parishes. A more thorough consideration of the various forms of incorporation which cannot be effected by local ordinaries will be discussed in the following article. For the present it will suffice to state that with the exception of the form of incorporation just mentioned above, that is to say, the union of a parish with the cathedral or with a collegiate church within the parish limits, all other forms of incorporation of parishes without an apostolic indult are forbidden to local ordinaries in the light of canon 1423, § 2.

Although, therefore, local ordinaries are forbidden by canon 1423, § 2, to unite a parish, that is, to amalgamate its revenues and income, with the mensal endowment *(mensa)* which serves the purpose of sustenance for the bishop or the cathedral chapter, they can, however, in virtue of the same paragraph of canon 1423 unite a parish with the cathedral or with a collegiate church

80 Cf. Pistocchi, *De Re Beneficiali,* pp. 89-90.

81 Canon 1420, § 3; *supra,* p. 69.

situated within the confines of the parish itself. The reason for this varied legislation is apparent. The local ordinary cannot unite a parish with the episcopal or capitular *mensa* lest he abuse his power to his own advantage.[82] A similar suspicion, however, would be devoid of any foundation if the advantage accruing from the union affected not the episcopal or capitular *mensa* but the cathedral or a collegiate church.[83]

The express purpose of the last clause of canon 1423 is to afford legislation to meet the needs of the cathedral or of a collegiate church. Its primary concern is, therefore, the welfare of the church itself, not that of the individuals attached thereto. In another part of its legislation the Code provides for the possible needs of these individuals. In cathedral and prominent collegiate chapters, where the prebends and distributions are so small that they do not suffice for the support of the canons, the bishop shall, with the advice of the chapter and upon obtaining the permission of the Holy See, unite some simple benefices with the canonries.[84] Canon 394, § 3, is, therefore, directly concerned with the welfare of the individual beneficiaries. Canon 1423, § 2, on the contrary, is *directly* concerned with the welfare of the cathedral or of a collegiate church as such, and only *indirectly* with the welfare of the individual beneficiaries. Canon 394, § 3, moreover, treats of the union of *simple benefices,* whereas canon 1423, § 2, deals with the union of *parishes.* Finally, the unions effected in favor of the cathedral or of a collegiate church are performed in virtue of the bishop's ordinary power; the union of simple benefices in favor of individual beneficiaries, on the other hand, cannot be performed without the express permission of the Holy See.

In effecting the incorporation mentioned in canon 1423, § 2, the local ordinary cannot, however, unite the cathedral or a collegiate church with any parish whatsoever. The words of the canon, *quae in territorio paroeciae sit,* would seem to require that only that parish be united within whose boundaries the cathedral

82 C. 2, *de rebus ecclesiae non alienandis,* III, 4, in Clem.

83 Pistocchi, *De Re Beneficiali,* p. 92.

84 Canon 394, § 3.

or collegiate church is situated. The local ordinary cannot, therefore, according to canon 1423, § 2, unite the cathedral or a collegiate church with any *other* parish, merely because it possesses a more substantial income.

Canon 1423, § 2, then, empowers the local ordinary to incorporate a parish with the cathedral or with a collegiate church situated within the parish limits. But what form of incorporation can he employ? Can the incorporation be effected either *ad temporalia tantum* or *pleno iure?* Vermeersch-Creusen maintain that the local ordinary is empowered under the provision of canon 1423, § 2, to incorporate a parish with the cathedral or a collegiate church within the parish boundaries simply *ad temporalia tantum.*[85] The reason for this restriction, they say, is to be found in the fact that canon 1423, § 2, allows the local ordinary to effect only that form of incorporation in which the *reditus* or income of the parish is ceded to the cathedral or collegiate church. It has been demonstrated in an earlier part of this work, however, that *only* the *reditus* or income, not the property itself *(bona ipsa)*, is ceded to the moral person whether the incorporation be effected *ad temporalia tantum* or *pleno iure.* Wherefore, the words *ut reditus paroeciae cedant in commodum ipsius ecclesiae* as employed in canon 1423, § 2, do not of themselves seem to exclude the possibility that the incorporation be effected *pleno iure* as well as *ad temporalia tantum.*

Blat[86] and Pistocchi,[87] on the other hand, interpret canon 1423, § 2, as empowering the local ordinary to effect the incorporation either *ad temporalia tantum* or *pleno iure.* This interpretation, it seems to the writer, is to be preferred. Canon 1423, § 2, in granting to the local ordinary power to incorporate a parish with the cathedral or with a collegiate church situated within the parish boundaries, prescribes that a suitable portion of the *fructus* or income of the parish is to be assigned to the

85 "Duplex unio ecclesiae cathedralis vel collegialis cum paroecia existere potest; . . . Prior unio sine indulto S. Sedis est invalida, altera ab episcopo pendet (c. 1423, § 2)." — *Epitome,* I, n. 539.

86 *Commentarium,* III, pars altera, n. 322, p. 399.

87 *De Re Beneficiali,* p. 93.

pastor or to the *vicar (relicta parocho vel vicario congrua portione)*. Now, according to canon 471, that cleric is known as the vicar *(vicarius)* who exercises the care of souls in a parish united *pleno iure* with a moral person.[88]

If, then, canon 1423, § 2, intended to restrict the local ordinary to effecting the incorporation of a parish with the cathedral or with a collegiate church *ad temporalia tantum,* would it not have omitted the word *vicario* which patently, according to canon 471, § 1, connotes the presence of a union effected *pleno iure?* Because of the employment of the words *"parocho vel vicario"* in canon 1423, § 2, therefore, the writer contends that the local ordinary can incorporate a parish with the cathedral or with a collegiate church situated within the parish boundaries either *ad temporalia tantum* or *pleno iure.*

Article 4. The Types of Union Forbidden to Local Ordinaries

Canon 1423, § 2. Nequeunt vero paroeciam unire cum mensa capitulari vel episcopali, cum monasteriis, ecclesiis religiosorum aut alia persona morali, neque cum dignitatibus et beneficiis ecclesiae cathedralis vel collegiatae . . .

Canon 1424. Ordinarii numquam possunt . . . unire . . . beneficia unius dioecesis cum beneficiis alterius diocesis, etiamsi ambae dioeceses aeque principaliter unitae ab uno Episcopo regantur; neque beneficia exempta vel Sedi Apostolicae reservata cum aliis quibuslibet.

In the preceding article consideration was given to those types of the union of parishes which can be effected by local ordinaries. The present article considers the types of union

[88] Canon 471, § 1. Si paroecia *pleno iure* fuerit unita domui religiosae, ecclesiae capitulari vel alii personae morali, debet constitui *vicarius,* qui actualem curam gerat animarum, assignata eidem congrua portione fructuum, arbitrio Episcopi.

which are expressly withdrawn from their competence. Local ordinaries are forbidden to unite a parish with the *mensa capitularis* or *episcopalis,* with monasteries, with churches of religious, or with another moral person, or, finally, with dignities or benefices of a cathedral or collegiate church.[89] Ordinaries, moreover, may not unite the benefices of one diocese with those of another diocese, even though both dioceses be co-ordinatively united and governed by but one bishop; nor can they unite exempt benefices or those which are reserved to the Holy See with any other benefices whatsoever.[90]

Section 1. Historical Development of These Prohibitions

Under the early law of the *Corpus Iuris Canonici* the competence of local ordinaries with regard to the union of parishes existed practically without limitation. Examination reveals that parishes were freely united with benefices and with other moral persons. Thus, in the Decretals Alexander III (1159-1181) gives evidence of how parishes were united with dignities and prebends of the cathedral church.[91] And again in another place Honorius III (1216-1227) in a letter to Robert, Bishop of Veszprém, in the year 1225, also speaks of uniting parish churches and chapels with prebends and dignities of the cathedral church.[92] At still a later date, as demonstrated by Clement V (1305-1314) in the Council of Vienne (1311-1312), bishops were still uniting parishes with other parishes, and with dignities and prebends of the cathedral church, as well as with religious houses.[93] In addition to these, parishes were also united by bishops with monasteries as well as with religious houses.[94]

89 Canon 1423, § 2.

90 Canon 1424.

91 C. 30, X, *de praebendis et dignitatibus,* III, 5.

92 C. 33, X, *de praebendis et dignitatibus,* III, 5; Potthast, *Regesta Pontificum Romanorum,* n. 7351.

93 "Si una ecclesia alteri ecclesiae, seu dignitati alicui vel praebendae per episcopum uniatur aut religioso loco donetur . . ." — c. 2, *de rebus ecclesiae non alienandis,* III, 4, in Clem.

94 C. 7, X, *de donationibus,* III, 24; c. 2, *de rebus ecclesiae non alienandis,* III, 4, in Clem.

The first limitation placed upon this extensive episcopal power seems to have been introduced by Clement V in the Council of Vienne (1311-1312), wherein bishops were forbidden to unite a parish with the episcopal *mensa* or with the *mensa* of the Chapter.[95] Evidently such a procedure had been permissible up until that time, for from the fact that Clement V used the word *decernimus* the Glossator came to the conclusion that the Pope thereby introduced a new provision into the law.[96] Commenting upon the entire content of the provision of Clement V, the Glossator attempted to find the reason underlying such a prohibition, and the reason he assigned was simply this: since neither the bishop alone nor the chapter alone could authorize anything in its own favor, *a fortiori* they could not do so by joint consent.[97]

With this single exception, the erstwhile power of bishops over the union of parishes endured up until the time of the Council of Trent. Therein this power was fundamentally confirmed. Indeed, not only was the ordinary power of the bishop conserved, but additional power from the Holy See was delegated to them in this matter.[98] But if the Council of Trent saw fit to confirm in general this power of the bishop, it also introduced some new restrictions.

In the first place, the Council of Trent forbade the union of the benefices of one diocese with those of another, and, consequently, also the union of the parishes of one diocese with those of another.[99] This enactment of the Council of Trent constituted

95 "Quod si episcopus (cui etiam capituli accedente consensu) mensae suae vel ipsi capitulo aliquam duxerit ecclesiam uniendam; hoc irritum esse decernimus et inane, contraria consuetudine non obstante." — c. 2, *de rebus ecclesiae non alienandis,* III, 4, in Clem.

96 *Glos. Ord.*, c. 2, *de rebus ecclesiae non alienandis,* III, 4, in Clem., s. v. *decernimus.*

97 *Glos. Ord., loc. cit.*

98 "Ut etiam Ecclesiarum status, ubi sacra Deo officia ministrantur ex dignitate conservetur, possint Episcopi, etiam tamquam Apostolicae Sedis delegati, iuxta formam iuris, sine tamen praeiudicio obtinentium facere uniones perpetuas quarumcumque Ecclesiarum parochialium . . ." — Conc. Trident., sess. XXI, *de ref.*, c. 5.

99 "Et quia iure optimo distinctae fuerunt dioeceses et parochiae, ac

a change in the law, for according to the common interpretation of the previous law bishops had the power to unite the benefices of their dioceses with those of another diocese, provided that the consent of the other bishop was obtained, since there was no provision in the law to the contrary.[100] This law of the Council of Trent endured through the years[101] up until its reception into the Code of Canon Law.[102]

In a later session the Council of Trent further restricted the right of bishops in the matter of the union of parishes. It has already been pointed out that in accord with pre-Tridentine law a bishop could unite parishes with monasteries, prebends and dignities of the cathedral church, as well as with religious houses.[103] Even in its earlier sessions the Council of Trent itself seems to have countenanced this state of affairs, for it contented itself with prescribing merely that bishops should annually visit the parish churches united in such a fashion.[104] It would seem, then, that up until the seventh session (March 3, 1547) of the Council of Trent no prohibition of this practice had as yet been issued. In the twenty-fourth session (November 11, 1563), however, the Council of Trent introduced some radical changes into the law. It expressly forbade bishops to unite parishes with monasteries, dignities and prebends of the cathedral or of a col-

unicuique gregi proprii attributi pastores . . . ut ordo ecclesiasticus non confundatur, aut una et eadem Ecclesia duarum quodammodo dioecesium fiat . . . beneficium unius dioecesis, etiamsi parochiales ecclesiae . . . alterius dioecesis beneficio, aut monasterio, seu collegio, vel loco etiam pio, perpetuo non uniantur." — Conc. Trident., sess. XIV, *de ref.*, c. 9.

100 Barbossa (1589-1649), *Collectanea Doctorum tam Veterum quam Recentiorum in Ius Pontificium Universum* (5 vols., Lugduni, 1669), lib. V, tit. VIII, n. 9; Garcia, *De Beneficiis*, pars XII, c. II, n. 85.

101 S. C. C., *Frisigen.*, 18 iun. 1735 — *Codicis Iuris Canonici Fontes cura Emi Petri Card. Gasparri Editi* (9 vols., Romae: Typis Polyglottis Vaticanis, 1923-1939. [Vols. VII, VIII et IX ed. *cura et studio Emi Iustiniani Card. Serédi*]), n. 3443.

102 Canon 1424.

103 *Supra*, p. 114.

104 "Beneficia ecclesiastica curata quae cathedralibus, collegiatis, seu aliis Ecclesiis, vel monasteriis, beneficiis, seu collegiis, aut piis locis quibuscumque unita et annexa reperiuntur, ab Ordinariis locorum annis singulis visitentur." — Conc. Trident., sess. VII, *de ref.*, c. 7.

legiate church, with any simple benefices, or with hospitals or with military orders.[105] This decree of the Council of Trent, as is apparent, was revolutionary in the restrictions it placed upon the power of the bishop. Moreover, it paved the way for the present-day legislation of the Code as found in canon 1423, § 2.

Although there is no explicit mention of the fact in the Council of Trent itself, nonetheless exempt benefices, too, remained outside the scope of competence of the local ordinary so far as the effecting of their union was concerned. This followed from the fact that exempt benefices were removed from his jurisdiction. In the old law, as in the new, the union of such benefices could be executed only by a special provision of the Holy See.[106]

Pre-Code legislation and the commentators thereupon generally conceded that it was within the bishop's power to unite benefices even if one of them was reserved.[107] The reason assigned by the commentators for this competence was derived in view of the nature of the reservation itself, for the reservation affected the title *(titulus)* of the benefice rather than its property *(proprietas)*. Wherefore, it was contended, if a benefice was reserved it was the title and not the property which was affected in and by its conferment. Accordingly, whether the benefice was or was not reserved, it remained within the power of the bishop to change or alter the property of the benefice. It was admitted that bishops had the power to unite benefices, and since reservations affected only the title and not the property of the benefice, the competence of the bishop remained unchanged so far as the union of that benefice was concerned, for its union was concerned primarily with the property of the benefice and not with its title.[108]

105 "In unionibus vero quibuslibet . . . Ecclesiae parochiales monasteriis quibuscumque, aut abbatiis, seu dignitatibus, sive praebendis Ecclesiae cathedralis, vel collegiatae, sive aliis beneficiis simplicibus, aut hospitalibus, militiisve non uniantur . . ." — Conc. Trident., sess. XXIV, *de ref.*, c. 13.

106 Reiffenstuel, lib. III, tit. XII, n. 55; Garcia, *De Beneficiis*, pars XII, cap. II, n. 62.

107 Fagnanus, *Commentaria Super Quinque Libros Decretalium*, lib. V, tit. XXXI, n. 22; Garcia, *De Beneficiis*, pars XII, cap. II, n. 9.

108 Fagnanus, *Commentaria Super Quinque Libros Decretalium*, *loc. cit.*

Three restrictions were, however, placed upon this right of the bishop:

a) When the union of a reserved benefice was executed, it was indeed sustained as valid; its effects, however, remained *suspended* until the reservation had been honored by the Holy See's appointment of an incumbent the first time the benefice was vacated subsequent to the union. Once this consummation of the reservation had taken place, then and only then did the union go into effect.[109]

b) The power of the bishop to unite reserved benefices was admitted only when the reservation concerned the *collatio beneficii,* not when it was reserved *dispositioni Romani Pontificis.* In the latter case the bishop had no power to unite such a reserved benefice. The reason assigned for this distinction was that the simple reservation *(reservatum collationi Romani Pontificis)* affected only the title of the benefice, leaving the disposition of its property by the bishop intact, whereas the reservation *dispositioni Romani Pontificis* was in itself wide enough to affect both the title and the property of the benefice. Hence, it was commonly maintained that the bishop could not unite a parish that had been reserved to the *disposition* of the Roman Pontiff. Garcia, however, maintained the contrary opinion.[110]

c) The bishop was, furthermore, powerless to unite reserved parishes if the reservation was not temporary but perpetual, for such a union would, in accord with what has already been stated, never realize its effect, since for each successive time that the benefice was vacated the reservation of itself would demand that the appointment of the incumbent for the first time be made by the Holy See.[111]

109 Rota Dec., 658 alias 6, *de rebus ecclesiae non alienandis, in antiq.:* "Dico quod unio fieri potest de beneficio reservato, quae tamen non habet suum effectum quin Papa conferat ratione suae reservationis factae, sed postea dum non vacabit in Curia dicta unio habebit suum effectum." — Quoted by Fagnanus, *op. cit.,* lib. V, tit. XXXI, n. 23.

110 *De Beneficiis,* pars XII, cap. II, n. 93.

111 Fagnanus, *op. cit.,* lib. V, tit. XXXI, n. 30; Garcia, *De Beneficiis,* pars XII, cap. II, n. 92; Schmalzgrueber, lib. V, tit. V, n. 72.

The Council of Trent subsequently confirmed the older law concerning the power of the bishop to unite reserved benefices, not only by recognizing his ordinary power in the matter, but by adding to it delegated jurisdiction from the Holy See.[112] By its legislation, moreover, it ended all controversy as to whether the bishop could unite benefices reserved to the *dispositio* as well as to the *collatio Romani Pontificis,* when it stated that the bishop could unite benefices *"reservata aut qualitercumque affecta"*.[113]

Finally, the Council of Trent reprobated the contention of the older authors that in the union of a reserved benefice the effects of the union were not realized immediately, but remained suspended until the Holy See had first appointed its incumbent. The Council of Trent, it would seem, considered the effects of the union as being realized as soon as the union itelf had been performed, for it decreed that such a union, once made, could not later be recalled.[114]

Section 2. Legislation in the Code of Canon Law

The Code in canons 1423, § 2, and 1424 has for the greater part embodied the provisions of the old law. Some opportune changes have, however, been introduced. It has already been stated in the foregoing pages that the *union* of parishes properly so-called has reference to the linking together of a parish with some other *benefice;* the *incorporation* of parishes, on the other hand, denotes the joining together of a parish with some other

112 "Ut etiam Ecclesiarum status, ubi sacra Deo officia ministrentur, ex dignitate conservetur, possint Episcopi etiam tamquam Apostolicae Sedis delegati . . . facere uniones perpetuas quarumcumque Ecclesiarum parochialium . . . etiam si dictae Ecclesiae vel beneficia essent generaliter vel specialiter *reservata,* aut *qualitercumque affecta."* — Conc. Trident., sess. XXI, *de ref.,* c. 5.

113 Conc. Trident., *loc. cit.*

114 ". . . Quae uniones non possint revocari, nec quoquomodo infringi, vigore cuiuscumque provisionis, etiam ex causa resignationis, aut derogationis, aut suspensionis." — Conc. Trident., sess. XXI, *de ref.,* c. 5.

moral person *which is not a benefice.*[115] Canon 1423, § 2, treats of both the union and the incorporation of parishes.

The Code has adopted from the old law the legislation of Clement V (1305-1314) which forbade the union of parishes with the *mensa episcopalis* or with the *mensa capitularis*. Since, however, the Code speaks of only the *mensa episcopalis* or *capitularis*, and not of the *episcopatus* or the *capitulum* itself, Pistocchi concludes that the prohibition extends simply to the union which is conceded *ad temporalia tantum,* and not the union which is effected *pleno iure.*[116] Such a position, it seems, is hardly tenable, for does not the *unio pleno iure* include within itself the *unio ad temporalia* in addition to the *unio ad spiritualia?* Granted, therefore, that at least the union which is conceded *ad temporalia tantum,* and which is the less odious of the two, is forbidden in canon 1423, § 2, is not the union of a parish which is effected *pleno iure* with the chapter also excluded by the same canon? Moreover, even though the union of a parish which is effected *pleno iure* with respect to the chapter may not be ruled out by a strict interpretation of the word *mensa* in canon 1423, § 2, the same canon, however, forbids the union of a parish with another moral person *(cum alia persona morali),* making no distinction whatever between the union which is conceded *ad temporalia* and the union which is effected *pleno iure.* But is the chapter not a moral person? Finally, as Pistocchi himself admits, the question is of academic rather than of practical import, for even though such a union were not forbidden in canon 1423, § 2, the Code states in canon 452 that without an apostolic indult a parish cannot be united *pleno iure* to a moral person.[117]

115 "Incorporatio differt a simplici unione quia uniuntur solum beneficia inter se; incorporantur vero beneficia cum alia etiam persona morali." — Coronata, *Institutiones Iuris Canonici*, II, n. 981, p. 374.

116 "In quo sedulo est advertendum, quod cum agitur de mensa episcopali vel capitulari, non autem de episcopatu vel capitulo, unio paroeciae potest intelligi prohibita, vi huius canonis, quoad temporalia tantum . . ." — *De Re Beneficiali*, p. 91.

117 "Ceterum, quoad personas morales in universum, unio paroeciae cum ipsis, *pleno iure,* iam a can. 452 reservatur Sedi Apostolicae." — *De Re Beneficiali*, p. 91.

The Code has amplified somewhat the prohibitions of the Council of Trent. As the Council of Trent, so, too, the Code has forbidden the bishop to unite parishes with prebends and dignities of the cathedral chapter. But whereas according to the law of the Council of Trent only the union of a parish with a monastery was forbidden,[118] the Code, while retaining the word *monasteriis,* has in addition forbidden the incorporation of a parish with the churches of religious whatsoever. Moreover, the Council of Trent had forbidden specifically the union of parishes with hospitals and military orders; the Code, however, has amplified this provision by forbidding the union of parishes not only with the moral persons mentioned specifically in canon 1423, § 2, but with any moral person whatsoever.[119]

Coronata is of the opinion that by reason of canon 1423, § 2, ordinaries can effect incorporations, even *pleno iure,* within the limits established by that canon.[120] Moreover, he states that to realize a true incorporation the union of a benefice may be had not only with a religious house or church, but also with a Seminary, hospital, etc.[121] While the writer is inclined to agree with the second statement, he takes exception to the first, since he fails to see how the two can be reconciled. Granted that incorporation signifies the union of a benefice with a religious house or church, with a hospital, or with a Seminary, etc., how can Coronata contend that ordinaries are empowered under the provisions of canon 1423, § 2, to effect incorporations, even *pleno iure?*

Perhaps this statement of Coronata is to be understood as a counterpart of his opinion that ordinaries can effect all forms of the union of benefices *other than parishes,* if these unions are

118 Conc. Trident., sess. XXIV, *de ref.*, c. 13.

119 Canon 1423, § 2. Nequent vero paroeciam unire cum . . . alia persona morali . . .

120 "Vi c. 1423, § 2, Ordinarii possunt incorporationes facere etiam pleno iure intra limites a canone statutos." — *Institutiones Iuris Canonici,* II, n. 980.

121 "Nec requiri videtur ut habeatur incorporatio ut unio fiat cum domo religiosa aut cum ecclesia, sed potest etiam fieri cum Seminaria, hospitali, etc." — Coronata, *Institutiones Iuris Canonici,* II, n. 981.

not expressly forbidden in canons 1422, 1423, § 2, and 1424, since the Code is presumed to have excepted from his competence only the forms of union mentioned therein.[122] If this be the correct interpretation for Coronata's statement, then from this restrictive viewpoint one can justify his doctrine that by reason of canon 1423, § 2, ordinaries can effect incorporations even *pleno iure,* for apart from the express exceptions enacted in canons 1422 and 1424 the law is silent as regards the power of bishops to unite benefices which are not of a parochial nature.[123] But if Coronata's statement is to be interpreted as implying the power of the bishop also to effect the incorporations of *parishes* in the same manner, then the writer fails to see its foundation in law.

The last clause of canon 1423, § 2, grants to the local ordinary the power to unite a parish with the cathedral or a collegiate church situated within the limits of the parish itself. This is, indeed, a true form of incorporation. Moreover, as has already been pointed out in the foregoing pages, the more common opinion attributes to the bishop the power to effect such incorporations either *ad temporalia tantum* or also *pleno iure.*[124] With this solitary exception, however, it can be stated that all other forms of the *incorporation* of *parishes* cannot be validly executed without an indult from the Apostolic See. Corroboration for this statement can be found in the Code itself wherein it is expressly stated that without an Apostolic indult a parish cannot be united *pleno iure* to a moral person in such a fashion that the moral person becomes vested with the title of pastor.[125]

Again, canon 1425 speaks of the incorporation of a parish with a religious house, be it conceded *ad temporalia tantum* or be

122 "Alias aliquas uniones canonibus 1422 et 1424 Codex expresse prohibet; quaeri hic potest utrum uniones illis concessionibus expressis non comprehensas, aut illis prohibitionibus non exclusas facere possit. Iuris veteris interpretationibus freti, affirmative respondemus, posse scilicet Ordinarium uniones non prohibitas intra suae potestatis ambitum facere, quam interpretationem Codex admittere videtur cum quod excludere vult exprimat." — *Institutiones Iuris Canonici,* II, n. 980, p. 372.

123 Cf. Blat, *Commentarium,* III, pars altera, n. 322, p. 400.

124 *Supra,* p. 111.

125 Canon 452.

it effected *pleno iure*, as being executed by the Holy See. Finally, canon 1423, § 2, itself, excepting the case wherein a parish is united with the cathedral or with a collegiate church within its confines, excludes all forms of the incorporation of *parishes* from the competence of the local ordinary. The canon prohibits expressly certain forms of incorporation, for example, the incorporation with a monastery or with a religious house. However, it does not stop there, but goes on to forbid the union of a parish with any other moral person whatsoever.[126] No distinction is made in canon 1423, § 2, between the incorporation conceded *ad temporalia tantum* and the incorporation effected *pleno iure*. The canon simply states that with the exception of the cathedral or a neighboring collegiate church, neither monasteries, nor the churches or religious, nor *any other moral persons* can have a parish incorporated with them. Hence it must be concluded that an indult from the Holy See is required for the incorporation of parishes with these juridical institutes, regardless of the specific nature of the incorporation.

What should be said concerning unions effected contrary to the provisions of canon 1423, § 2? Are they invalid or merely illicit? The writer contends that they are invalid. The union of parishes involves the exercise of jurisdiction in the external forum. Now, when in canon 1423, § 1, it is stated that local ordinaries can *(possunt)* effect certain forms of the union of parishes, their jurisdiction in the matter is thereby confirmed. But when, on the other hand, in paragraph 2 of the same canon it is also stated that they cannot *(nequeunt)* accomplish certain other forms of union, it seems that the jurisdiction required for such unions is thereby denied to them. Unions effected without the proper jurisdiction, however, must be considered as invalid. The word *nequeunt* of canon 1423, § 2, therefore, must be interpreted, in the opinion of the writer, as stating *equivalently* that all actions performed contrary to this canon's prescriptions are invalid.[127]

126 Canon 1423, § 2. Nequeunt vero paroeciam unire cum . . . alia persona morali . . .

127 Canon 11.

The Code states expressly that ordinaries can never unite the benefices of one diocese with those of another, *even if* the dioceses in question be joined together by way of a co-ordinative union.[128] There are three possible cases in which this provision of the Code might find its application. The dioceses in question may not be united at all; secondly, they may be joined together by way of a subordinative union; finally, they may be joined together by means of a co-ordinative union. In any of the three cases, however, ordinaries are expressly forbidden to unite the benefices of one diocese with those of another. Coronata maintains that since the Code forbids these unions only *if* the dioceses are united by way of a *co-ordinative* union, such unions of benefices are not beyond the competence of the local ordinary if the dioceses are united by way of an *extinctive* or a *subordinative* union.[129]

Such an opinion, however, seems to be entirely without foundation if the words of canon 1424 are carefully considered. In the first place, if the dioceses have been united *extinctively*, there can be no place for the application of canon 1424 which forbids the union of the benefices of one diocese with those of another. Subsequent to an extinctive union there no longer remain *two* dioceses to which its provisions can be applied. One diocese alone remains, and the union of its benefices will then be governed by the provisions of canons 1422 and 1423, §§ 1, 2. Secondly, the Code does not forbid such unions *only if* the dioceses are co-ordinatively united, but *even if* such be their status. The words employed in canon 1424 are not *"si" dioeceses unitae sint aeque principaliter*, but *"etiamsi" dioeceses unitae sint aeque principaliter*.

Moreover, Coronata himself admits that canon 1424 is to be

128 Canon 1424. Ordinarii numquam possunt . . . unire . . . beneficia unius dioecesis cum beneficiis alterius dioecesis, etiamsi ambae dioeceses aeque principaliter unitae ab uno Episcopo regantur . . .

129 "Codex prohibet uniri beneficia dioeceseon unitarum si dioeceses unitae sint aeque principaliter, qui casus facile occurit; si tamen dioeceses uniantur per subiectionem aut extinctionem, unio non videtur prohibita." —*Institutiones Iuris Canonici*, II, n. 980, p. 373.

interpreted according to the old law, since it is nothing other than the old law incorporated into the Code of Canon Law.[130] Now, the very purpose which the Council of Trent had in mind in forbidding the union of the benefices of one diocese with those of another was to avoid both confusion in ecclesiastical discipline, and the possibility that one and the same church might pertain to two distinct dioceses, to the consequent detriment of its subjects.[131] Such a union could easily confuse the income destined for different parishes, and would require a troublesome separation should the union be later dissolved.[132] But could not such confusion arise just as easily from a subordinative union as from a co-ordinative union? Finally, the co-ordinative union is by far the least odious form of union. When, therefore, the Code forbids the union of the benefices of one diocese with those of another *even if (etiamsi)* the union between the two dioceses puts them on a co-ordinative basis, does it not *a fortiori* exclude the same type of union if the dioceses be subordinatively united?

Finally, canon 1424 states that ordinaries can never unite benefices which are reserved to the Holy See with any other benefice whatsoever. As demonstrated above, the Council of Trent had not only confirmed the ordinary power of bishops to unite reserved benefices, but had in addition rendered them delegates of the Holy See in this matter.[133] The Code, however, in canon 1424 has revoked both ordinary and delegated jurisdiction. The benefices reserved by law to the Holy See are enumerated in canon 1435.

Haydt maintains that this provision of canon 1424 is but a logical consequence of the nature and purpose of the reservation

130 "Quae hoc canone statuuntur iam iure vetere vigebant, ex illo proinde interpretationem accipiunt." — *Institutiones Iuris Canonici*, II, n. 980; cf. also, Blat, *Commentarium*, III, n. 323, p. 401.

131 ". . . ut ordo ecclesiasticus non confundatur, aut una et eadem Ecclesia duarum quodammodo diocesium fiat, non sine gravi eorum incommodo qui illi subditi fuerint: beneficia unius diocesis, etiamsi parochiales Ecclesiae . . . alterius diocesis beneficio . . . non uniantur . . ." — Conc. Trident., sess. XIV, *de ref.*, c. 9.

132 Vermeersch-Creusen, *Epitome*, II, n. 754.

133 Conc. Trident., sess. XXI, *de ref.*, c. 5.

itself.[134] He further maintains "that even the strong terminology of canon 1424, 'Ordinarii numquam possunt', does not necessarily decree the invalidity of acts against this canon.' "[135]

It appears to the writer, however, that the words *"numquam possunt"* of canon 1424 can well be interpreted as stating *equivalently* the invalidity of such acts in accord with the provision of canon 11. But if not from canon 1424 itself, certainly it would seem that from canon 1434 such invalidity can be established. Canon 1434 states that benefices reserved to the Holy See are invalidly conferred by inferiors thereto. It requires more power, however, to unite a benefice than it does to confer one. Wherefore, it would seem that, at least implicitly, the invalidity of such unions is established in canon 1434.[136]

134 "The reservation, it will be recalled, withdraws the benefice from the power of the local Ordinary and thus appropriates for the Apostolic See the exclusive right of conferring that benefice. Now, if the local Ordinary were free to unite this reserved benefice with another, he could, at least in an indirect manner, weaken the acquired right by uniting with the reserved benefice a benefice with an insufficient revenue. It is to avoid such infringements upon the acquired right of the Holy See that the Code forbids the local Ordinaries to unite any reserved benefices." — *Reserved Benefices*, The Catholic University of America Canon Law Studies, n. 161 (Washington, D. C.: The Catholic University of America Press, 1942), pp. 76-77; cf. also, Blat, *Commentarium*, III, 401; Augustine, *A Commentary on the New Code of Canon Law*, VI, 504.

135 *Reserved Benefices, loc. cit.*

136 Pistocchi, *De Re Beneficiali*, p. 99; Blat, *Commentarium*, III, 401; Haydt, *Reserved Benefices*, p. 77.

CHAPTER SIX

SOLEMNITIES TO BE OBSERVED IN THE UNION OF PARISHES

A modification in the original status of any benefice whatsoever is a matter of concern to the Church as a whole. But if this is true of benefices in general, it is especially true when the modification is to affect a canonical parish, for the welfare of souls has ever been the prime concern of the Church in its legislation. Accordingly, though the legislator has seen fit to empower local ordinaries to effect certain forms of the union of parishes, he has at the same time been unwilling that this power should be limitless. Numerous considerations have made it imperative that this power should be burdened with certain definite restrictions.

In the first place, since any union of parishes is considered in law as odious, the matter should not be placed entirely at the option of the bishop. Some definite canonical cause should exist to justify the exercise of this power. Secondly, it is quite possible that during the time that the parishes existed as separate, independent juridical entities certain persons may have obtained acquired rights therein. Now it would certainly be contrary to natural equity were the local ordinary permitted to unite parishes with utter disregard for the acquired rights of others.

Realizing the importance of these considerations, the Code in granting to local ordinaries power to execute the union of parishes has ordered them to observe certain legal solemnities. Three solemnities are, therefore, to be considered as essential to the union of parishes: first, there must be present a proved canonical cause; secondly, all interested parties are to be cited before proceeding to the union; finally, the assistance of the cathedral chapter is to be employed.[1]

1 Canons 1423, §1; 1424; 1428, §1.

It would be erroneous to suppose that this legislation of the Code is new legislation. True, certain points in the law do occur for the first time in the Code, but in general it can be stated that the law of the Code concerning these solemnities is substantially the same as the law of the Decretals and that of the Council of Trent.[2] Decisions of the Sacred Congregation of the Council based upon the old law witness the necessity of all three solemnities.[3] It is to be noted, however, that the prescribed solemnities were to be observed by bishops, not necessarily by the Roman Pontiff.[4]

Thus far the discussion has been centered about the necessity of these solemnities in general. It will now be expedient to consider each solemnity in a separate article. Since, however, the law itself was established at a very early date, and has remained in great part unchanged upon its incorporation into the Code, one shall necessarily have to seek out its interpretation particularly from its application to practical cases by the Sacred Congregation of the Council and from the works of pre-Code authors.

2 C. 33, X, *de praebendis et dignitatibus*, III, 5; c. un., *de statu monachorum*, III, 10, in Clem.; c. 7, X, *de donationibus*, III, 24; c. 2, *de rebus ecclesiae non alienandis*, III, 4, in Clem; Conc. Trident., sess. VII, *de ref.*, c. 6; Conc. Trident., sess. XXIV, *de ref.*, c. 15. Cf. also, Mendoza, *De Beneficiorum Incompatibilitate atque Compatibilitate* (Venetiis, 1579), pars II, cap. 3, nn. 8-10; Garcia, *De Beneficiis*, pars XII, cap. II, nn. 108-126, 145-220; Pirhing, *Jus Canonicum*, lib. III, tit. V, nn. 208-11; Reiffenstuel, lib. III, tit. XII, nn. 67-83; Schmalzgrueber, lib. III, tit. V, nn. 199-200; 202.

3 S. C. C., *Feretrana*, 24 apr. 1847, § *Secunda:* "Sed si unio fiat ab Episcopo insuper necessaria est discretio . . . qua disquiritur num vere adsit canonica necessitatis aut utilitatis causa; quae disquisitio fieri debet in Capitulo . . . Capituli consensum suppleri solet a Sede Apostolica vel Sacra hac Congregatione. . . . Necessaria deinde est vocatio eorum, quorum intersit, et nominatim patronorum quorum si consensio desit unionem irritam esse tradit Lotterius." — *Thes. Resol.*, CVII, 277.

4 S. C. C., *Urbevetana*, 6 mart. 1819, § *Agitur* — *Thes. Resol.*, LXXIX, 67; S. C. C., *Feretrana*, 24 apr. 1847, § *Si autem* — *Thes. Resol.*, CVII, 277.

Article 1. The Existence and Establishment of the Canonical Cause

Canon 1423, § 1. Ordinarii locorum . . . possunt . . . ob Ecclesiae necessitatem vel magnam et evidentem utilitatem, aeque aut minus principaliter unire quaslibet paroeciales ecclesias inter se aut cum beneficio non curato . . .

Canon 1428, § 2. Unio . . . facta sine canonica causa irrita est.

Canon 1428, § 3. Adversus decretum Ordinarii unientis . . . datur in devolutivo tantum recursus ad Sanctam Sedem.

Canon 1423, § 1, expressly establishes the canonical causes for the union of parishes when it states that local ordinaries can effect certain forms of unions because of the necessity or the great and evident utility of the Church. The canonical causes for the union of parishes are, therefore, two: the *necessity* and the *utility* of the Church.

Honorius III, in 1225, authoritatively established necessity or utility as the specific canonical causes for the union of benefices.[5] The Council of Trent in turn reiterated the preceding law, insisting that unions executed for any other cause were invalid.[6] During the course of the years the Sacred Congregation of the Council applied the law as established by Honorius III, permitting the union of parishes if the canonical causes were present.[7] Moreover, the same Sacred Congregation repeatedly forbade such unions under pain of nullity if the canonical causes

[5] "Si evidens necessitas vel utilitas exigat, praebendis ecclesiae tuae poteris de capellis in perpetuum annectendis eisdem . . . augmentare . . ." — c. 33, X, *de praebendis et dignitatibus*, III, 5.

[6] Conc. Trident., sess. VII, *de ref.*, c. 6.

[7] S. C. C., *Eugubina*, 19 dec. 1801, § *Tridentinum* — *Thes. Resol.*, LXVII, 311; S. C. C., *Fesulana*, 13 ian. 1816, § *Siquidem:* "Siquidem beneficiorum unio, quae secumfert voluntatis commutationem, ex censura Tridentini non alio modo concedenda est, quam si constiterit de rationabili causa, quae aut necessitatem vel utilitatem Ecclesiae respiciat. . . ." — *Thes. Resol.*, LXVII,

were not present.[8] The law of canon 1423, § 1, is but an incorporation of the preceding law into the Code of Canon Law.

Necessity and utility are assigned in canon 1423, § 1, as the canonical causes for the union of parishes. These terms are, however, rather general and hence seem to require an ulterior determination. In other words, what conditions in the state of a parish constitute a case of *necessity* for its union with another? What conditions render such a union *useful?*

A true case of necessity can certainly be said to exist when the revenues of the parishes whose union is contemplated become insufficient to support their incumbents.[9] It often happens that parishes which for many years were self-supporting later begin to deteriorate. Several factors may be responsible for this deterioration. Thus, the white population often tends to recede from a certain locality because of the influx of the colored.[10] It may also happen that the abandonment of some industrial project, which had given employment to a considerable number of the parishioners, causes them to seek employment in another locality. Whatever the cause, such migration generally results in the financial failure of the parish originally established in that locality. Should, therefore, the bishop ascertain that for any reason whatsoever a parish is unable to cope with its financial obligations, there would certainly seem to be present a valid cause of necessity for his uniting that parish with some other

4; S. C. C., *Florentina,* 18 mart. 1820, § *Verumtamen — Thes. Resol.,* LXXX, 89.

8 S. C. C., *Saleritana,* 21 nov. 1739, § *Multiplici — Thes. Resol.,* IX, 133; S. C. C., *Aversana,* 12 iul., 23 aug. 1755 — *Thes. Resol.,* XIX, 76, 91; S. C. C., *Tolentinaten.,* 17 dec. 1808 — Pallottini, *Collectio Omnium Conclusionum et Resolutionum Congregationis Concilii ab anno 1564-1860* (18 vols., Romae, 1868-1893), III, v. *beneficia,* n. 226; S. C. C., *Ravennaten.,* 1 mart. 1817, § *Confratres — Thes. Resol.,* LXXVII, 69; S. C. C., *Reatina,* 19 dec. 1818, § *Agitur — Thes. Resol.,* LXXVII, 310.

9 ". . . possint Episcopi facere uniones perpetuas quarumcumque Ecclesiarum parochialium . . . propter earum paupertatem. . . ." — Con. Trident., sess. XXI, *de ref.,* c. 5; *Glos. Ord.,* c. 3, C. X, q. 3, s. v. *necessitate;* Pistocchi, *De Re Beneficiali,* p. 87.

10 Augustine, *The Canonical and Civil Status of Catholic Parishes in the United States,* p. 152.

parish. Or perhaps by uniting two parishes in similar circumstances, one self-supporting parish can be realized.

A decrease in population may in itself be sufficient to constitute a further cause for uniting two parishes.[11] Such a situation will generally be linked with the resultant poverty of the parish, so that both conditions go together to constitute a cause of necessity. However, it is quite possible that these two causes may not co-exist. It may well be that so far as finances are concerned, stable endowments assure a successful continuation of the parish. The number of people attached thereto, however, may be so small that it becomes impossible, or at least impracticable, to assign a pastor to so few people. In such a case the bishop would be empowered to unite this parish with a more extensive one.

The destruction or utter desolation of the parish church may well afford a third cause of necessity for the union of parishes.[12] Thus, if the church of a certain parish has been destroyed by fire and it is found impossible to erect another in its stead, the bishop can proceed to unite this parish with some other parish still in possession of its church. It is to be noted, however, that necessity for uniting the two parishes can scarcely be alleged if the parishioners are willing to remove the cause of necessity by financing the construction of a new church.[13]

Examples of cases containing great and evident *utility* are rather rare in the sources and older authors. Several causes of utility can, however, be assigned as reasonably justifying the union of parishes. Thus, the welfare of souls, the proximity of parish churches in those locales where one parish would certainly suffice, and, finally, a great saving of expenses can justify the union of parishes among themselves.[14] In the opinion of the writer, another evident case of utility would exist in those dioceses

11 Barbosa, *Juris Ecclesiastici Universi*, lib. III, cap. XVI, n. 38; Coronata, *Institutiones Iuris Canonici*, III, n. 980, p. 372.

12 C. 49, C. XVI, q. 1.

13 Rossi, *De Paroecia*, p. 39.

14 Augustine, *The Canonical and Civil Status of Catholic Parishes in the United States*, p. 152.

in which the bishop has not at his disposal a number of priests sufficient or equipped to assume the office of pastor.

The writer has attempted to give some examples of situations which may well constitute cases of necessity or utility. He does not pretend, however, that this is a taxative enumeration of all possible cases. Ultimately, therefore, the decision as to the necessity or utility of the union will rest with the local ordinary to determine in each individual instance. Since, however, the law in canon 1428, § 3, explicitly affords the remedy of recourse *in devolutivo* to the Holy See, it will be advisable for the ordinary to assure himself that a proportionately grave cause of necessity or utility actually exists before he proceeds to the union, in order that he may be spared the possible if not also likely embarrassment of having his decision reversed by the Holy See because of the lack of a true canonical cause.

Thus far the discussion has concerned the necessity of the *existence* of the canonical cause. However, it was not considered sufficient merely to assert the presence of the cause, but an investigation was required to determine and to prove that such a cause was really present. This is what was known in the old law as the *establishment* of the canonical cause, or, technically, the *cognitio causae*. All authors were in accord on this point of law.[15] Moreover, the Sacred Congregation of the Council was wont to require the establishment or proving of the existence of the canonical cause to exclude any shadow of doubt.[16] The Code makes no explicit mention of the necessity of such a juridical establishment of the cause. Since, however, the legislation of the Code on this point is nothing other than that of the old law, it appears that in virtue of canon 6, 2°, such a procedure is still required even under the law of the Code.[17]

15 Garcia, *De Beneficiis*, pars XII, cap. II, n. 120; Barbosa, *Juris Ecclesiastici Universi Libri Tres* (Lugdini, 1660), lib. III, cap. 16, n. 39; Pirhing, *Jus Canonicum*, lib. III, tit. V, n. 210; Reiffenstuel, lib. III, tit. XII, n. 67; Schmalzgrueber, lib. III, tit. V, n. 182. Cf. also, Wernz-Vidal, *Ius Canonicum*, II, n. 172.

16 S. C. C., *Basileen.*, 26 mart. 1768 — *Thes. Resol.*, XXXVII, 68; S. C. C., *Feretrana*, 24 apr. 1847 — *Thes. Resol.*, CVII, 276.

17 Cf. Wernz-Vidal, *Ius Canonicum*, II, n. 172.

It is, however, by no means necessary that the establishment of the canonical cause assume the form of a judicial trial, since the union of parishes has to do with the exercise of administrative and not judicial power. An extra-judicial, summary process will suffice. It is not necessary that the ordinary himself conduct the investigation, but he may delegate whomsoever he pleases. He may well enlist the services of the rural dean to investigate the condition of a parish situated within the confines of his district.

Finally, canon 1428, § 2, states that a union effected without a canonical cause is invalid. Wherefore, though the Code in canon 1423, § 1, has committed a great deal to the judgment of the ordinary when it states in general terms that *necessity* or *utility* are the canonical causes for union, still canon 1428, § 2, emphasizes the fact that the existence and establishment of *some* canonical cause is a matter of no small importance. The ordinary is to decide whether definite circumstances in the condition of a parish constitute a cause of necessity or utility. Some such cause, however, must actually be present, for otherwise the entire transaction will be null and void.

A discussion existed among pre-Code authors as to the efficacy of a union effected by reason of a false cause or no cause at all. All authors were in accord in establishing the nullity of such a union. Some, however, maintained that the union was *ipso facto* null and void, and needed no declaration to that effect.[18] This nullity is what Vermeersch-Creusen call *nullitas plenissima*.[19] Others, on the contrary, maintained that the union, though null and void, needed a declaration to that effect, and until such a declaration was made by a higher authority, a bishop could not confer either of the benefices which his predecessor had united with the contention that the union had been

18 Garcia, *De Beneficiis*, pars XII, cap. II, n. 13; Reiffenstuel, lib. III, tit. XII, n. 71; Schmalzgrueber, lib. III, tit. V, n. 181; De Angelis, *Praelectiones Iuris Canonici*, lib. III, tit. V, n. 26.

19 "Nullitas distinguitur plenissima, quae ipso iure, sine ulla sententia operatur. . . ." — *Epitome*, I, n. 102, 2.

executed with a false cause or no cause at all.[20] Nullity of this type is called *minus plena*.[21]

It appears that the Code in canon 1428, § 2, has sanctioned the latter of these two opinions. It states merely that a union executed without a canonical cause is invalid. Paragraph 3 of the same canon, however, states that recourse is granted, but *in devolutivo tantum.* Wherefore, the decree of the ordinary whereby two parishes are united must be considered as having realized its effect, notwithstanding the fact that recourse has been interposed, until a declaration to the contrary is issued by the Holy See.[22] Recourse, if desired, must be sought with the Sacred Congregation of the Council.[23] Moreover, the primary purpose of the legislator in canon 1423, § 1, seems to have been to expedite the fruitful administration of parishes. It would, however, only serve to create confusion and would defeat the very purpose of the law were the decree of union of the ordinary to remain suspended each time recourse against his action was made to the Holy See. Accordingly, it can be stated that though a union effected without canonical cause is, indeed, invalid, the decision of the ordinary must stand and must be observed until it has been rescinded by the Holy See.

Article 2. The Citation of Interested Parties

Canon 1424. Ordinarii numquam possunt beneficia quaevis unire sive curata sive non curata, cum detrimento eorum qui eadem actu obtinent, ipsis invitis; neque beneficium iuris patronatus cum beneficio liberae collationis sine patronorum consensu; . . .

Canon 1428, § 1. Locorum Ordinarii uniones . . . ne faciant nisi per authenticam scripturam, auditis . . . iis,

20 Mendoza, *De Beneficiorum Incompatibilitate atque Compatibilitate,* pars II, cap. 3, n. 17; cf. also, Reiffenstuel, lib. III, tit. XII, n. 71.

21 Vermeersch-Creusen, *Epitome,* I, n. 102, 2.

22 Canon 1889, §1; cf. Pistocchi, *De Re Beneficiali,* p. 135.

23 Canon 250; §2.

si qui sint, quorum intersit, praesertim rectoribus ecclesiarum.

Canon 1424 states that ordinaries can never unite benefices, whether or not the care of souls be attached to them, to the detriment of those who are actually in possession of the benefices at the time the union is effected, if they be unwilling to suffer said detriment. In accord with this canon, therefore, ordinaries cannot unite two parishes when the union involves an injustice to either of the pastors, if the pastor under consideration is unwilling to accept any infringement of his rights. If, however, there be an actual, objective infringement of these rights, but the pastor is willing to accept such detriment, then the union of the parishes is not forbidden by reason of canon 1424.

Canon 1428, § 1, states that ordinaries should not execute the union of benefices without the *advice* of those who have an interest therein. Now, the pastor in actual possession of the parish whose union with another parish is under contemplation is most certainly an interested party. Accordingly, at least his *advice* in the matter must be sought, though it need not necessarily be followed.[24]

Canon 1428, § 1, seems to treat of unions in general, with no reference whatsoever as to whether or not the union involves a detriment to one or other of the beneficiaries. Canon 1424, on the other hand, considers the specific case in which some detriment would be suffered by at least one incumbent should the union be actually effected. If such be the case, canon 1424 seems to require more than the mere *advice* of the pastor as is required in canon 1428, § 1. Canon 1424 states that ordinaries cannot unite benefices whether these exist with or without the annexed care of souls, to the detriment of those who are in actual possession thereof, if they be unwilling to suffer such detriment. It appears to the writer that, to effect a union involving a detriment to one or other of the present incumbents, *consent* to accept the detriment must first be obtained. Moreover, in accord with

[24] Canon 105, 1°.

canon 105, 1°, failure to obtain such *consent* invalidates the union.

It is to be noted, however, that the consent of the actual pastor is required not for the union itself, but rather to suffer the detriment deriving therefrom. If, therefore, a way has been found to *remove* any detriment deriving from the union, the pastor cannot oppose it in virtue of canon 1424, since consent cannot be required for that which does not exist. Now, any form of the union of parishes necessarily involves a diminution in the number of benefices at the disposal of the ordinary. Subsequent to the union of two parishes there will be place for but one pastor, whereas previously there was place for two. Accordingly, one of the pastors must necessarily lose his parish precisely because of the union. But if the ordinary has offered to transfer the pastor thus deprived of his parish to a parish of equal or superior merit, such a pastor can scarcely be said to suffer a detriment because of the union. If such a transfer be offered the pastor, the union would in no wise entail an objective detriment to his rights, even though he be reluctant to accept the new parish which has been offered to him. Wherefore, such a union, it appears, would not be forbidden in virtue of canon 1424.

Irremovable pastors, however, cannot be transferred without their consent unless special faculties have been received from the Holy See.[25] Consequently, should it become desirable to unite a parish which has as its incumbent an irremovable pastor, and the pastor, declining a transfer, opposes the union on the contention that it would be effected to his detriment, it appears to the writer that the only juridical solution for the problem would be either to obtain faculties from the Holy See in order to compel his transfer, or to await that time when the benefice shall have been vacated, and then proceed to its union.

The present-day legislation of the Code patently favors the voluntary renunciation of the right of patronage.[26] Moreover,

25 Canon 2163, § 1.

26 Canon 1451, § 1.

it explicitly forbids the bestowal of such a right for the future.[27] However, in the event that the patron is unwilling to renounce his right of patronage, the Church has every intention of protecting that acquired right.[28] Now, if a benefice to which is attached the right of patronage were without the consent of the patron united to another benefice in respect of which the appointment of the incumbent is a matter of free disposition for the ordinary, the patron's right would necessarily suffer some detriment. In an extinctive union, according to the enactment of canon 1420, the very right of patronage would itself be extinguished. In a mutually co-ordinative or in a collaterally subordinative union, the right would on the other hand be restricted, for the one and sole rector would be subject to the free nomination of the ordinary on the one side, and to the right of patronage on the other. The right of the ordinary as well as that of the patron would then be restricted. Indeed, they would be in conflict one with the other. Accordingly, canon 1424 states that ordinaries can never unite a benefice in respect of which the appointment of the incumbent is a matter of free disposition with a benefice to which is attached the right of patronage without the *consent* of the patron.

Here again canon 1424 seems to require more than does canon 1428, § 1. Patrons most certainly are to be included under the provision of canon 1428, § 1, which requires seeking the *advice* of interested parties in the union of benefices. According to canon 1424, however, the obtaining of *advice* is not sufficient, but *consent* is required before the ordinary can proceed to unite with another benefice in respect of which the appointment can be made freely a benefice to which is attached the right of patronage. Should the patron give his consent, the union can be lawfully effected. The right of patronage is extinguished, however, if, with the consent of the patron, the benefice to which was attached his right of patronage is united with another for which the appointment remains an altogether free act on the part of the

27 Canon 1450, § 1.

28 Canons 4; 1451, § 2.

ordinary.[29] If, on the contrary, the patron refuses his consent, the ordinary cannot unite the benefices, since the consent of the patron is necessary for the valid union of the parishes in question.[30]

The provision of canon 1424 which requires the consent of the patron — and this for validity in accord with canon 105, 1° — is in full accord with the prescriptions of the old law. The Council of Trent stated that it was unjust to violate the acquired rights of patrons.[31] Moreover, it cautioned ordinaries that the consent of the patron was to be obtained in the union of benefices.[32] Finally, unions effected without this consent were considered as null and void.[33]

It appears, therefore, when there is question of a patron or of an actual beneficiary who is to suffer some detriment to his rights, that *consent* must be obtained before the union of the parishes can be validly effected. By reason of canon 1428, § 1, however, it is sufficient to have the *advice* of all other interested parties. This provision had already been established in the old law.[34] Indeed, at times the practice of the Sacred Congregation of the Council seems to to have required their *consent*.[35]

The Code, however, in canon 1428, § 1, has contented itself with requiring the mere *advice* of interested parties. Thus,

29 Canon 1470, § 1, 5°.

30 Canon 105, 1°. Si consensus exigatur, Superior contra earundem personarum votum invalide agit. Cf. also, Blat, *Commentarium,* III, n. 323; Coronata, *Institutiones Iuris Canonici,* II, n. 980, p. 373; Vermeersch-Creusen, *Epitome,* II, n. 754; Pistocchi, *De Re Beneficiali,* p. 94.

31 "Legitima patronatuum iura tollere . . . aequum non est. . . ." — Conc. Trident., sess. XXV, *de ref.,* c. 9.

32 ". . . liceat Episcopis . . . aliquot simplicia beneficia . . . unire . . . cum patronorum consensu. . . ." — Conc. Trident., sess. XXIV, *de ref.,* c. 15.

33 Conc. Trident., sess. VII, *de ref.,* c. 6.

34 "Quod omnes tangit, debet ab omnibus approbari." — Reg. 29, R. J., in VI°; Conc. Trident., sess. VII, *de ref.,* c. 6; S. C. C., *Fesulana,* 13 ian. 1816, § *Siquidem — Thes. Resol.,* LXXVI, 4.

35 S. C. C., *Eugubina,* 19 dec. 1801, § *Tridentinum — Thes. Resol.,* LXVII, 311; S. C. C., *Nullius,* 17 maii 1828 — Pallottini, *Collectio Omnium Conclusionum et Resolutionum Congregationis Concilii,* III, v. *beneficia,* n. 209.

though there be no question of an infringement upon his rights, still the pastor must be called to give his advice before the ordinary proceeds to effect a union between his parish and another parish. This requirement of the law seems altogether logical, for who other than the pastor is better qualified to advise the ordinary concerning the presence of the necessary canonical cause? Moreover, natural equity seems to demand that a particular benefactor who has been exceptionally generous in his contributions towards the parish be considered an interested party and consequently be summoned to offer his advice in the matter.[36] Pre-Code authors as well as post-Code authors, however, have been in perfect harmony in stating that there is no requirement in law to summon the parishioners of the parish which is to be united.[37] At most it can be stated that should the people have a serious objection to the union, it will be *advisable* to hear them. There is, however, no obligation imposed by law to do so.

It has already been stated above that the *advice* of interested parties is all that is required by canon 1428, § 1. But is the obtaining of this advice to be considered as necessary for the validity of the action, or merely for its lawfulness? The answer seems to rest upon the interpretation given to canon 105, 1°.[38] If the words *"satis est ad valide agendum"* of canon 105, 1°, be interpreted as requiring advice in order to act *validly*, then it follows that the unions of parishes executed without the advice of the interested parties are invalid. But if these words be in-

36 Connolly, *The Canonical Erection of Parishes*, pp. 65-66.

37 Mendoza, *De Beneficiorum Incompatibilitate atque Compatibilitate*, pars II, cap. III, n. 9; Garcia, *De Beneficiis*, pars XII, cap. II, nn. 219 220; Reiffenstuel, lib. III, tit. XII, n. 76; Coronata, *Institutiones Iuris Canonici*, II, 373; Blat, *Commentarium*, III, n. 327; Connolly, *op. cit.*, p. 65.

38 Canon 105, 1°. Cum ius statuit Superiorem ad agendum indigere consensu vel consilio aliquarum personarum:

1° Si consensus exigatur, Superior contra earundem votum invalide agit; si consilium tantum, per verba, ex. gr.: *de consilio consultorum*, vel *audito Capitulo, parocho*, etc., satis est ad valide agendum ut Superior illas personas audiat; . . .

terpreted as merely positing a condition for the lawfulness of the action, then such unions would be merely illicit.

From the promulgation of the Code up until the present time a controversy has existed among authors concerning the correct interpretation of canon 105, 1°.[39] The majority of authors, among them Ojetti,[40] Chelodi,[41] De Meester,[42] Maroto,[43] Blat,[44] Coronata,[45] and Goyeneche,[46] interpret canon 105, 1°, as requiring the seeking of counsel on the part of the superior in order that he may act validly.[47] And yet, the arguments advanced by those who hold the contrary view, foremost among whom are Vermeersch-Creusen,[48] Boudinhon,[49] and Creusen,[50] are cogent enough to lend to this opinion at least extrinsic probability.[51]

While it appears to the writer that the text and context of canon 105, 1°, seem to indicate that actions performed without the prescribed consultation are *invalid,* notwithstanding the dire consequences of such an interpretation — for one is concerned here with a matter of law and not of convenience — still, *for practical purposes,* in view of the solid probability of the con-

39 For a detailed study of this controversy, cf. Bastnagel, *The Appointment of Parochial Adjutants and Assistants,* pp. 206-228.

40 *Commentarium in Codicem Iuris Canonici* (4 vols., Romae: Universitas Gregoriana, 1927-1931), II, 180-185, 186-202.

41 *Ius de Personis* (2. ed., Tridenti, 1927), nn. 102, 231 b, footnote 3, pp. 180, 383-384.

42 *Juris Canonici et Juris Canonico-Civilis Compendium,* II, n. 879, p. 339.

43 *Institutiones Iuris Canonici,* I, n. 471, p. 555.

44 *Commentarium,* II, nn. 36, 526, pp. 45, 516.

45 *Institutiones Iuris Canonici,* I, n. 153, p. 172, footnote 8.

46 *Juris Canonici Summa Principia* (Roma: Tip. Pol. "Cuore di Maria," 1935), p. 144.

47 For a more complete citation of authors in support of this opinion, cf. Bastnagel, *op. cit.,* pp. 225-226.

48 *Epitome,* I, n. 197 bis, pp. 151-152.

49 "An nullus semper sit actus Superioris non petito consilio," — *Jus Pontificium* (Romae, 1921-), VIII (1928), 29-35.

50 "L'effet juridique des consultations," — *Nouvelle Revue Théologique* (Paris, 1869-), LV (1928), 100-116.

51 A more complete citation of the authors who favor this opinion can be found in Bastnagel, *op. cit.,* p. 227.

trary opinion, he hesitates to label as invalid those unions of parishes which have been executed or which may be executed when the advice of the interested parties has not been obtained. Wherefore, until that time when perhaps an authentic interpretation will have definitely put an end to the controversy, it seems *safe* to call such unions merely *illicit* in accord with the norms of canons 11 and 15, and to conclude with Bastnagel that "it seems indicated to acknowledge the extrinsic probability of the less common opinion, and hence, not to be disturbed about the consequences of acts which superiors might execute in violation of the demand of canon 105, 1°."[52]

Article 3. The Intervention of the Cathedral Chapter

Canon 1428. § 1. Locorum Ordinarii uniones . . . ne faciant nisi per authenticam scripturam, auditis Capitulo cathedrali et iis, si qui sunt, quorum intersit . . .

The requirements of the law concerning the parties interested in a particular union of parishes have already been discussed in the preceding article. It now remains but to consider what the law has established concerning the intervention of the cathedral chapter. The requirements of the Code in this matter are less stringent than were those of the old law. The law of the Decretals consistently required the *consent* of the cathedral chapter in order that the bishop might validly execute the union of parishes.[53] The Council of Trent in turn reaffirmed the necessity of such consent.[54] Subsequent decisions of the Sacred Congregation of the Council, moreover, showed the application of this law to practical cases.[55] Still other decisions of the same Sacred

52 *The Appointment of Parochial Adjutants and Assistants*, p. 228.

53 "Sed ut Episcopi donatio (seu unio Ecclesiae pio loco facta) sit legitima, consensus est sui Capituli requirendus." — c. 7, X, *de donationibus*, III, 24; c. 2, *de rebus Ecclesiae non alienandis*, III, 4, in Clem.

54 ". . . liceat Episcopis unire quaedam beneficia cum consensu capituli. . . ." — Conc. Trident., sess. XXIV, *de ref.*, c. 15.

55 S. C. C., *Ferrarien.*, 3 maii 1594: ". . . posse Episcopum erigere

Congregation demonstrate that this consent was required in order that the union of benefices be *validly* performed.[56]

The Code of Canon Law, however, has introduced a change in the law, for according to canon 1428, § 1, the *advice* and no longer the *consent* of the cathedral chapter is all that is required for the union of benefices. Moreover, it is not required that the ordinary heed their advice, but it is sufficient that the cathedral chapter (diocesan consultors where in accord with canon 427 they supply for the chapter) be heard.[57] This consultation is to be made with the chapter or consultors as a group and not as individuals, and ordinaries are cautioned to give grave consideration to their opinion in the matter, and not to depart therefrom without a sufficiently grave reason.[58] In mission countries the vicar or prefect apostolic before proceeding to the union of quasi-parishes should obtain the counsel of the three advisors mentioned in canon 302. According to this canon, however, it is not necessary that they be heard as a group, but it is sufficient that their advice be stated in writing.

Here again it may be asked whether unions of parishes executed without the proper consultation of the cathedral chapter are to be considered as invalid or merely illicit. Once more the solution to the problem seems to depend upon the interpretation given to canon 105, 1°. The writer is inclined to establish such unions as invalid. In view of what has already been stated, however, and until an authentic interpretation has definitely

Parochialem illique sic erectam de consensu capituli unire beneficium." — Pallottini, *Collectio Omnium Conclusionum et Resolutionum Congregationis Concilii*, III, v. *beneficia*, n. 226; S. C. C., *Ferrarien.*, 3 maii 1594 — Pallottini, *op. cit.*, III, v. *beneficia*, n. 225.

56 S. C. C., *Nullius*, mense iul. 1597: "Omissio consensus Capituli in unione Beneficiorum simplicium seu curatorum cum curatis, reddit nullam unionem." — Pallottini, *op. cit.*, v. *beneficia*, n. 223; S. C. C., *Nullius*, mense iul. 1597: ". . . in unionibus Beneficiorum simplicium vel curatorum cum curatis, adhibendum esse consensum Capituli, eoque praeterito, nullas esse uniones." — Pallottini, *op. cit.*, v. *beneficia*, n. 224; S. C. C., *Basileen.*, 26 mart. 1768 — *Thes. Resol.*, XXXVII, 68.

57 Canon 105, 1°.

58 Canon 105, 1°, 2°.

terminated the controversy, it seems safe to say that *in practice* such unions *can be* considered as merely *illicit.*[59]

Article 4. Necessity and Nature of the Document of Union

Canon 1428, § 1, further requires that an authentic document be executed whenever two benefices are united. This requirement of the Code constitutes, as it were, a fourth solemnity. It was not unknown in the old law, but was not ordinarily enumerated among the usual solemnities.[60] The document will be *authentic* when it is drawn up by an ecclesiastical notary in accord with the provisions of canon 374, §§ 1, 2, and signed by the ordinary responsible for the union.[61] Thus, should the property rights of the new parish resulting from the union be later assailed in an ecclesiastical trial, this instrument will have the force of a public document.[62]

The document should contain an accurate account of the entire transaction, viz.: the identity of the parishes involved; the canonical cause for the union; the name of the ecclesiastical superior effecting the union; the type of union intended by that superior; mention as to whether the chapter, consultors, or other interested persons have been cited; and finally, an indication of the place, day, month, and year wherein the document is drawn up.[63]

But what juridical effect would the failure to draw up this document have upon the union itself. Pistocchi states in no uncertain terms that in such a case the union itself would be *invalid,* since the execution of the document is necessary for the validity of the entire transaction.[64] In this rather singular

59 Cf. *supra,* pp. 139-140.

60 Cf. S. C. C., *Feretrana,* 24 apr. 1847 — *Thes. Resol.,* CVII, 277.

61 Coronata, *Institutiones Iuris Canonici,* II, n. 979, p. 370; Pistocchi, *De Re Beneficiali,* p. 130.

62 Canon 1813, §1, 1°, 2°.

63 Coronata, *Institutiones Iuris Canonici, loc. cit.*

64 "Haec solemnitas est certe ad *validitatem;* agitur enim de actu con-

opinion Pistocchi seems to confuse the *decree* of union with the *proof* thereof in the external forum, for the document as such does not effect the union, but merely gives evidence that such has been performed.[65]

Most certainly, the union of benefices must be performed by a legitimate ecclesiastical authority, since it involves the constitution of a new benefice.[66] This is done by the decree of the ordinary. The decree of the superior is admittedly, therefore, necessary for validity. It does not follow, however, that the the *document* containing that decree is likewise necessary for validity. The words of canon 1428, § 1, *ne faciant nisi per authenticam scripturam,* contain a very definite prescription as to the manner in which the union is to be executed; but in accord with canon 11 they do not seem to constitute an equivalent statement of invalidity. Wherefore, the writer prefers to adhere to the opinion of the majority of authors according to which this document is required not for validity but merely for lawfullness.[67]

stitutivo novi negotii, per Ordinarium, circa *erectum* beneficium peragendi." —*De Re Beneficiali,* p. 130.

65 Connolly *(The Canonical Erection of Parishes,* p. 72) makes a similar distinction between the *decree* of erection and *document* of erection.

66 Canon 1414, §§ 2, 3.

67 Blat, *Commentarium,* lib. II, partes II-VI, n. 327, p. 407; Augustine, *A Commentary on the New Code of Canon Law,* VI, 512; Cocchi, *Commentarium,* III, n. 104, p. 228; Wernz-Vidal, *Ius Canonicum,* II, n. 172, p. 194.

PARTICULAR CONCLUSIONS

1. An extinctive union is to be enumerated among the possible modes for the erection of parishes.

2. Granted that the decree of incorporation issued by the Holy See in a particular case may decree otherwise, the legislation of the Code, however, seems to indicate clearly that a parish even after its union with a religious house, if effected *ad temporalia tantum* or also *pleno iure*, remains a *subiectum iuris*, and therefore retains ownership or dominion of all its property. Accordingly, all the property pertaining to the parish *(bona ipsa)* must not be amalgamated with that pertaining to the religious house to which it is united either *ad temporalia tantum* or *pleno iure;* a separate administration for both types of property seems to be required by the Code.

3. Vicars and prefects apostolic, with reference to the union of *quasi-parishes,* enjoy the same competence as that accorded by the Code to local ordinaries with reference to the union of *parishes.*

4. The union, as effected by the local ordinary, of a parish with the cathedral church or with a collegiate church situated within the parish boundaries, either *ad temporalia tantum* or *pleno iure*, is a true form of incorporation. The incorporation of a parish with any other moral person, however, whether it be effected *ad temporalia tantum* or *pleno iure,* cannot be validly executed by the local ordinary without an indult from the Holy See.

5. In executing the union of parishes, *consultation* with the interested parties will generally suffice. When, however, there is question of a patron or of an actual beneficiary who would suffer some detriment to his rights, the local ordinary must obtain their *consent* to unite the parishes in which their acquired rights are founded.

6. So long as the controversy concerning the correct interpretation of canon 105, 1°, endures, unions of parishes executed without the *advice* of the cathedral chapter (diocesan consultors) and of interested parties are, *in practice,* to be considered as *valid*, but *illicit.*

BIBLIOGRAPHY

Sources

Acta Apostolicae Sedis, Commentarium Officiale, Romae, 1909—.

Canones et Decreta Sacrosancti et Oecumenici Concilii Tridentini, Parisiis, 1754.

Codex Iuris Canonici Pii X Pontificis Maximi iussu digestus Benedicti Papae XV auctoritate promulgatus, Romae: Typis Polyglottis Vaticanis, 1917. Reimpressio, 1936.

Codicis Iuris Canonici Fontes cura Emi. Petri Card. Gasparri Editi, 9 vols., Romae: Typis Polyglottis Vaticanis, 1923-1939. (Vols. VII, VIII, et IX ed. *cura et studio Emi Iustiniani Card. Serédi.)*

Collectanea S. Congregationis de Propaganda Fide, 2 vols, Romae, 1907.

Corpus Iuris Canonici, ed. Lipsiensis 2, post Aemilii Ludovici Richteri curas instruxit Aemilius Friedberg, 2 vols., Lipsiae: Ex officina Bernhardi Tauchnitz, 1879-1881. Editio anastatice repetita, Lipsiae: Tauchnitz, 1928.

Decretales D. Gregorii Papae IX suae integritati una cum glossis restitutae, Romae, 1582.

Decretum Gratiani Emendatum et Notationibus Illustratum una cum Glossis, Gregorii XIII Pont. Max., iussu Editum, 2 vols., Romae, 1582.

Jaffé, Philippus, *Regesta Pontificum Romanorum ab condita Ecclesia ad annum post Christum natum MCXCVIII*, 2. ed. correctam et auctam auspiciis Gulielmi Wattenbach curaverunt S. Loewenfeld, F. Kaltenbrunner, P. Ewald, 2 vols. in 1, Lipsiae, 1885-1888.

Journel, M. J. Rouët de, *Enchiridion Patristicum*, 11. ed., Friburgi Brisgoviae: Herder and Co., 1937.

Liber Sextus Decretalium D. Bonifatii Papae VIII, suae integritati una cum Clementinis et Extravagantibus earumque Glossis restitutus, Romae, 1582.

Pallottini, Salvator, *Collectio Omnium Conclusionum et Resolutionum Congregationis Concilii ab anno 1564-1860*, 18 vols., Romae, 1868-1893.

Potthast, Augustus, *Regesta Pontificum Romanorum inde ab anno post Christum natum MCXCVIII ad annum MCCCIV*, 2 vols., Berolini, 1874-1875.

Quinque Compilationes Antiquae necnon Collectio canonum Lipsiensis, ad librorum manu scriptorum fidem recognovit et adnotatione critica instruxit Aemilius Friedburg, Lipsiae, 1882.

Thesaurus Resolutionum Sacrae Congregationis Concilii, 167 vols., Romae, 1718-1908.

AUTHORS

Aichner, Simon, *Compendium Juris Ecclesiastici*, 6. ed., Brixinae, 1887.

(Bachofen), Charles Augustine, *A Commentary on the New Code of Canon Law*, 8 vols., Vol. VI, 2. ed., St. Louis: B. Herder, 1923.

———, *The Canonical and Civil Status of Catholic Parishes in the United States*, St. Louis: B. Herder Book Co., 1926.

Barbosa, Augustinus, *Collectanea Doctorum tam Veterum quam Recentiorum in Jus Pontificium Universum*, 5 vols., Lugdini, 1669.

———, *Juris Ecclesiastici Universi Tres*, Lugdini, 1660.

Bastnagel, Clement, *The Appointment of Parochial Adjutants and Assistants*, The Catholic University of America Canon Law Studies, n. 58, Washington, D. C.: The Catholic University of America, 1930.

Blat, Albertus, *Commentarium Textus Codicis Iuris Canonici*, 5 vols. in 6, Romae: ex Typographia Pontificia in Instituto Pii IX, 1921-1927.

Bouix, Dominicus, *Tractatus de Parocho*, Parisiis, 1855.

Bouscaren, T. Lincoln, *Canon Law Digest*, 2 vols. (Vol. I, 1934, Vol. II, 1943), Milwaukee: The Bruce Publishing Co., 1934-1943.

Chelodi, Ioannes, *Ius de Personis*, 2. ed., Tridenti, 1927.

Coady, John, *The Appointment of Pastors*, The Catholic University of America Canon Law Studies, n. 52, Washington, D. C.: The Catholic University of America, 1929.

Cocchi, Guidus, *Commentarium in Codicem Iuris Canonici*, 5 vols. in 8, Vol. V, 3. ed. (1932), Taurinorum Augustae: Marietti, 1931-1938.

Connolly, Nicholas, *The Canonical Erection of Parishes*, The Catholic University of America Canon law Studies, n. 114, Washington, D. C.: The Catholic University of America, 1938.

Coronata, Matthaeus Conte a, *Institutiones Iuris Canonici*, 5 vols., Taurini: Marietti, 1928-1936.

Craisson, D., *Manuale Totius Juris Canonici*, 6. ed., 4 vols., Patavii, 1880.

De Angelis, Philippus, *Praelectiones Iuris Canonici*, 5 vols., Romae, 1908.

De Luca, Joannes Card., *Theatrum Veritatis et Justitiae*, 15 vols. in 8 and Index, Coloniae Agrippinae, 1706.

De Meester, A., *Juris Canonici et Juris Canonico-Civilis Compendium*, ed. nova, 3 vols. in 4, Brugis: Desclée, 1921-1928.

Devoti, Joannes, *Institutionum Canonicarum Libri IV*, 4 vols., ed. septima Romana, Romae, 1829.

Donnellan, Thomas, *The Obligation of the* MISSA PRO POPULO, The Catholic University of America Canon Law Studies, n. 155, Washington, D. C.: The Catholic University of America Press, 1942.

Engel, Ludovicus, *Collegium Universi Juris Canonici*, 9. ed., Beneventi, 1760.

Fagnanus, Prosperus, *Commentaria Super Quinque Libros Decretalium*, 5 vols., Romae, 1661.

Fanfani, P. Ludovicus, *De Iure Parochorum ad Norman Codicis Iuris Canonici*, Romae: Marietti, 1924.

Ferrari, Joseph C., *Summa Institutionum Canonicarum*, 3. ed., 2 vols., Januae, 1877.

Ferraris, F. Lucius, *Bibliotheca Canonica Iuridica Moralis Theologica necnon Ascetica Polemica Rubristica Historica*, 9 vols., Romae, 1885-1899.

Garcia, Nicholas, *De Beneficiis Ecclesiasticis Amplissimus et Doctissimus Tractatus*, Venetiis, 1618.

Gasparri, Petrus, *De Matrimonio*, ed. nova, 2 vols., Romae: Typis Polyglottis Vaticanis, 1932.

Golden, Henry Francis, *Parochial Benefices in the New Code*, The Catholic University of America Canon Law Studies, n. 10, Washington, D. C.: The Catholic University of America, 1925.

Goyeneche, S., *Juris Canonici Summa Principia*, Romae: Tip. Pol. "Cuore de Maria," 1935.

Haydt, John Joseph, *Reserved Benefices*, The Catholic University of America Canon Law Studies, n. 161, Washington, D. C.: The Catholic University of America Press, 1942.

Hostiensis, Cardinalis (Henricus de Segusio), *Commentaria in Quinque Decretalium Libros*, 5 vols. in 3, Venetiis, 1581.

———, *Summa Aurea*, Lugduni, 1568.

Laurentius, Joseph, *Institutiones Iuris Ecclesiastici*, Friburgi Brisgoviae, 1903.

Lombardi, Carolus, *Iuris Canonici Privati Institutiones*, 2. ed., 3 vols., Romae, 1910.

Maroto, Philippus, *Institutiones Iuris Canonici*, 2 vols., Matriti, 1919.

McDonough, Thomas, *Apostolic Administrators*, The Catholic University of America Canon Law Studies, n. 139, Washington, D. C.: The Catholic University of America Press, 1941.

Mendoza, Alonso, Hojeda de, *De Beneficiorum Incompatibilitate atque Compatibilitate*, Venetiis, 1579.

Migne, J. P., *Patrologiae Cursus Completus, Series Graeca*, 161 vols., Parisiis, 1856-1866.

Ojetti, Benedict, *Commentarium in Codicem Iuris Canonici*, 4 vols., Romae: Universitas Gregoriana, 1927-1931.

Pirhing, Ernricus, *Jus Canonicum in Quinque Libros Decretalium Distributum*, 5 vols., Dilingae, 1722.

Pistocchi, Marius, *De Re Beneficiali iuxta Canones*, Taurini: Marietti, 1928.

Prümmer, Dominicus M., *Manuale Iuris Ecclesiastici*, ed. altera, 2 vols., Friburgi Brisgoviae, 1920.

Rebuffus, Pertus, *Praxis Beneficiorum*, Venetiis, 1610.

Reiffenstuel, Anacletus, *Jus Canonicum Universum*, 6 vols., Romae, 1831-1834.

Reilly, Edward, *The General Norms of Dispensation*, The Catholic University of America Canon Law Studies, n. 119, Washington, D. C.: The Catholic University of America Press, 1939.

Rossi, Joseph, *De Paroecia*, Romae, 1923.

Sanguinetti, Sebastiano, *Iuris Ecclesiastici Privati Institutiones*, Romae, 1884.

Santi, Franciscus, *Praelectiones Juris Canonici*, 4. ed. (Martin Leitner), 3 vols., Romae, 1903-1905.

Schmalzgrueber, Franciscus, *Jus Ecclesiasticum Universum*, 5 vols. in 12, Romae, 1943-1845.

Suarez, Franciscus, *Opera Omnia*, ed. nova, 26 vols. et 2 Indices, Parisiis, 1856-1866.

Thiel, Andreas, *Epistolae Romanorum Pontificum a S. Hilario usque ad S. Hormisdam*, Brunsbergae, 1868.

Thomassinus, Ludovicus, *Vetus et Nova Ecclesiae Disciplina*, 3 vols., Parisiis, 1688.

Vermeersch, A.—Creusen, J., *Epitome Iuris Canonici*, 3 vols., Romae: Dessain, Vol. I, 6. ed., 1937; Vol. II, 5. ed., 1934; Vol. III, 5. ed., 1936.

Vromant, G., *De Bonis Ecclesiae Temporalibus*, Louvain: Desbarax, 1927.

Wernz, F. X., *Ius Decretalium*, 3. ed., 6 vols., Prati, 1913-1914.

Wernz, F.—Vidal P., *Ius Canonicum ad Codicis Normam Exactum*, 7 vols. in 8, Romae: Aedes Universitatis Gregorianae, 1923-1938.

Winslow, Francis Joseph, *Vicars and Prefects Apostolic*, The Catholic University of America Canon Law Studies, n. 24, Washington, D. C.: The Catholic University of America, 1924.

Woywod, S., *A Practical Commentary on the Code of Canon Law*, 6th printing, 2 vols., New York: Joseph F. Wagner, 1941.

Articles

Bondini, A., "Circa il rendiconto del parroco religioso al Vescovo,"—*Il Monitore Ecclesiastico*, XXXVIII (1926), 335-347.

d'Angelo, Sosius, "Il Codice di Diritto Canonico,"—*Il Monitore Ecclesiastico*, XXXII (1920), 288-290.

Dooley, Eugene, "The Juridical Status of the Parishes of Religious: Another View,"—*The Jurist*, III, 117-128.

Goyeneche, S., "Consultationes,"—*Commentarium pro Religiosis*, X (1929), 39-44, 177-183.

Hannan, Jerome, "The Juridical Status of the Parishes of the Religious,"—*The Jurist*, I, 329-335.

Kinane, J., "The Obligation of Parish Priests to Apply Their Superfluous Revenues to the Poor and to Pious Uses"—*Irish Ecclesiastical Record*, 5. Series, 1913—XXVIII (1926), 639-642.

McReavy, Lawrence L., "Parochial Benefices in England and Wales"—*The Clergy Review*, XV (1938), 189-202; 376; 468-470; 562-564; XVI (1939), 84-88; 275-280.

Nebreda, Eulogius, "Quaestiones Selectae de Iure Administrativo Ecclesiastico"—*Commentarium pro Religiosis*, VII (1926), 107-118, 191-198, 261-271, 317-333.

Nevin, J., "Are Parishes in Australia Benefices?"—*Australasian Catholic Record*, VII (1930), 172-174.

Vidal, P., "Il Nuovo Codice di Diritto Canonico"—*Civiltà Cattolica*, LIX (1918), 309-312.

PERIODICALS

Australasian Catholic Record, The, Manly, 1923—.

Civiltà Cattolica, La, Roma, 1850—.

Clergy Review, The, London, 1931—.

Commentarium pro Religiosis (from 1935, *Commentarium pro Religiosis et Missionariis)*, Romae, 1920—.

Irish Ecclesiastical Record, The, Dublin, 1864—.

Jurist, The, Washington, D. C., 1941—.

Jus Pontificium, Romae, 1921—.

Monitore Ecclesiastico, Il, Roma, 1876—.

Nouvelle Revue Théologique, La, Paris, 1869—.

LIST OF ABBREVIATIONS

AAS—Acta Apostolicae Sedis.

C. I. C.—Codex Iuris Canonici.

Collectanea—Collectanea Sacrae Congregationis de Propaganda Fide.

Conc. Trident.—Concilium Tridentinum.

CpR[M]—*Commentarium pro Religiosis et Missionariis.*

Fontes—Codicis Iuris Canonici Fontes.

Glos. Ord.—Glossa Ordinaria.

Loc. cit.—Loco citato.

Op. cit.—Opere citato.

R. J.—Regulae Juris.

S. C. C.—Sacra Congregatio Concilii.

S. C. de Prop. Fide—Sacra Congregatio de Propaganda Fide.

S. Poenit. Ap.—Sacra Poenitentiaria Apostolica.

ANALYTICAL INDEX

BIOGRAPHICAL NOTE

Thomas M. Mundy was born on October 19, 1914, at Tamaqua, Pennsylvania. He attended St. Canicus' Parochial School, Mahanoy City, Pennsylvania, and was graduated from the Mahanoy City Public High School in June of 1932. In the fall of that year he was admitted into the Archdiocesan Seminary of St. Charles Borromeo, Philadelphia, where he completed his preparatory studies and his course in Philosophy. In August of 1937 he was sent by the Cardinal Archbishop to pursue his Theological Studies in the Pontifical Roman Seminary, Rome, Italy. He received the degree S.T.B. from the Pontificio Ateneo Lateranense in May of 1940. The following September he entered the Catholic University of America where he was ordained to the priesthood, December 20, 1940, and received the degree S.T.L. in May of 1941. In the fall of 1941 he enrolled in the School of Canon Law at the Catholic University where he received the degrees J.C.B. and J.C.L. in the years 1942 and 1943 respectively.

CANON LAW STUDIES*

1. FRERIKS, REV. CELESTINE A., C.PP.S., J.C.D., Religious Congregations in Their External Relations, 121 pp., 1916.
2. GALLIHER, REV. DANIEL M., O.P., J.C.D., Canonical Elections, 117 pp., 1917.
3. BORKOWSKI, REV. AURELIUS L., O.F.M., J.C.D., De Confraternitatibus Ecclesiasticis, 136 pp., 1918.
4. CASTILLO, REV. CAYO, J.C.D., Disertacion Historico-Canonica sobre la Potestad del Cabildo en Sede Vacante o Impedida del Vicario Capitular, 99 pp., 1919 (1918).
5. KUBELBECK, REV. WILLIAM J., S.T.B., J.C.D., The Sacred Penitentiaria and Its Relation to Faculties of Ordinaries and Priests, 129 pp., 1918.
6. PETROVITS, REV. JOSEPH, J.C., S.T.D., J.C.D., The New Church Law on Matrimony, X-461 pp., 1919.
7. HICKEY, REV. JOHN J., S.T.B., J.C.D., Irregularities and Simple Impediments in the New Code of Canon Law, 100 pp., 1920.
8. KLEKOTKA, REV. PETER J., S.T.B., J.C.D., Diocesan Consultors, 179 pp., 1920.
9. WANENMACHER, REV. FRANCIS, J.C.D., The Evidence in Ecclesiastical Procedure Affecting the Marriage Bond, 1920 (Printed 1935).
10. GOLDEN, REV. HENRY FRANCIS, J.C.D., Parochial Benefices in the New Code, IV-119 pp., 1921 (Printed 1925).
11. KOUDELKA, REV. CHARLES J., J.C.D., Pastors, Their Rights and Duties According to the New Code of Canon Law, 211 pp., 1921.
12. MELO, REV. ANTONIUS, O.F.M., J.C.D., De Exemptione Regularium, X-188 pp., 1921.
13. SCHAAF, REV. VALENTINE THEODORE, O.F.M., S.T.B., J.C.D., The Cloister, X-180 pp., 1921.
14. BURKE, REV. THOMAS JOSEPH, S.T.D., J.C.D., Competence in Ecclesiastical Tribunals, IV-117 pp., 1922.
15. LEECH, REV. GEORGE LEO, J.C.D., A Comparative Study of the Constitution "Apostolicae Sedis" and the "Codex Juris Canonici," 179 pp., 1922.
16. MOTRY, REV. HUBERT LOUIS, S.T.D., J.C.D., Diocesan Faculties According to the Code of Canon Law, II-167 pp., 1922.
17. MURPHY, REV. GEORGE LAWRENCE, J.C.D., Delinquencies and Penalties in the Administration and the Reception of the Sacraments, IV-121 pp., 1923.

* Below n. 100 only the following numbers are still available: Nn. 3, 4, 9, 25, 34, 57 and 75. Beginning with n. 100 only the following are unavailable: Nn. 100-111, inclusive, and n. 113.

18. O'Reilly, Rev. John Anthony, S.T.B., J.C.D., Ecclesiastical Sepulture in the New Code of Canon Law, II-129 pp., 1923.
19. Michalicka, Rev. Wenceslas Cyril, O.S.B., J.C.D., Judicial Procedure in Dismissal of Clerical Exempt Religious, 107 pp., 1923.
20. Dargin, Rev. Edward Vincent, S.T.B., J.C.D., Reserved Cases According to the Code of Canon Law, IV-103 pp., 1924.
21. Godfrey, Rev. John A., S.T.B., J.C.D., The Right of Patronage According to the Code of Canon Law, 153 pp., 1924.
22. Hagedorn, Rev. Francis Edward, J.C.D., General Legislation on Indulgences, II-154 pp., 1924.
23. King, Rev. James Ignatius, J.C.D., The Administration of the Sacraments to Dying Non-Catholics, V-141 pp., 1924.
24. Winslow, Rev. Francis Joseph, O.F.M., J.C.D., Vicars and Prefects Apostolic, IV-149 pp., 1924.
25. Correa, Rev. Jose Servelion, S.T.L., J.C.D., La Potestad Legislativa de la Iglesia Catolica, IV-127 pp., 1925.
26. Dugan, Rev. Henry Francis, A.M., J.C.D., The Judiciary Department of the Diocesan Curia, 87 pp., 1925.
27. Keller, Rev. Charles Frederick, S.T.B., J.C.D., Mass Stipends, 167 pp., 1925.
28. Paschang, Rev. John Linus, J.C.D., The Sacramentals According to the Code of Canon Law, 129 pp., 1925.
29. Piontek, Rev. Cyrillus, O.F.M., S.T.B., J.C.D., De Indulto Exclaustrationis necnon Saecularizationis, XIII-289 pp., 1925.
30. Kearney, Rev. Richard Joseph, S.T.B., J.C.D., Sponsors at Baptism According to the Code of Canon Law, IV-127 pp. 1925.
31. Bartlett, Rev. Chester Joseph, A.M., LL.B., J.C.D., The Tenure of Parochial Property in the United States of America, V-108 pp., 1926.
32. Kilker, Rev. Adrian Jerome, J.C.D., Extreme Unction, V-425 pp., 1926.
33. McCormick, Rev. Robert Emmet, J.C.D., Confessors of Religious, VIII-266 pp., 1926.
34. Miller, Rev. Newton Thomas, J.C.D., Founded Masses According to the Code of Canon Law, VII-93 pp., 1926.
35. Roelker, Rev. Edward G., S.T.D., J.C.D., Principles of Privilege According to the Code of Canon Law, XI-166 pp., 1926.
36. Bakalarczyk, Rev. Richardus, M.I.C., J.U.D., De Novitiatu, VIII-208 pp., 1927.
37. Pizzuti, Rev. Lawrence, O.F.M., J.U.L., De Parochis Religiosis, 1927. (Not Printed).
38. Bliley, Rev. Nicholas Martin, O.S.B., J.C.D., Altars According to the Code of Canon Law, XIX-132 pp., 1927.
39. Brown, Mr. Brendan Francis, A.B., LL.M., J.U.D., The Canonical

Juristic Personality with Special Reference to its Status in the United States of America, V-212 pp., 1927.

40. Cavanaugh, Rev. William Thomas, C.P., J.U.D., The Reservation of the Blessed Sacrament, VIII-101 pp., 1927.
41. Doheny, Rev. William J., C.S.C., A.B., J.U.D., Church Property: Modes of Acquisition, X-118 pp., 1927.
42. Feldhaus, Rev. Aloysius H., C.PP.S., J.C.D., Oratories, IX-141 pp., 1927.
43. Kelly, Rev. James Patrick, A.B., J.C.D., The Jurisdiction of the Simple Confessor, X-208 pp., 1927.
44. Neuberger, Rev. Nicholas J., J.C.D., Canon 6 or the Relation of the Codex Juris Canonici to the Preceding Legislation, V-95 pp., 1927.
45. O'Keefe, Rev. Gerald Michael, J.C.D., Matrimonial Dispensations, Powers of Bishops, Priests, and Confessors, VIII-232 pp., 1927.
46. Quigley, Rev. Joseph A. M., A.B., J.C.D., Condemned Societies, 139 pp., 1927.
47. Zaplotnik, Rev. Johannes Leo, J.C.D., De Vicariis Foraneis, X-142 pp., 1927.
48. Duskie, Rev. John Aloysius, A.B., J.C.D., The Canonical Status of the Orientals in the United States, VIII-196 pp., 1928.
49. Hyland, Rev. Francis Edward, J.C.D., Excommunication, Its Nature, Historical Development and Effects, VIII-181 pp., 1928.
50. Reinmann, Rev. Gerald Joseph, O.M.C., J.C.D., The Third Order Secular of Saint Francis, 201 pp., 1928.
51. Schenk, Rev. Francis J., J.C.D., The Matrimonal Impediments of Mixed Religion and Disparity of Cult, XVI-318 pp., 1929.
52. Coady, Rev. John Joseph, S.T.D., J.U.D., A.M., The Appointment of Pastors, VIII-150 pp., 1929.
53. Kay, Rev. Thomas Henry, J.C.D., Competence in Matrimonial Procedure, VIII-164 pp., 1929.
54. Turner, Rev. Sidney Joseph, C.P., J.U.D., The Vow of Poverty, XLIX-217 pp., 1929.
55. Kearney, Rev. Raymond A., A.B., S.T.D., J.C.D., The Principles of Delegation, VII-149 pp., 1929.
56. Conran, Rev. Edward James, A.B., J.C.D., The Interdict, V-163 pp., 1930.
57. O'Neil, Rev. William H., J.C.D., Papal Rescripts of Favor, VII-218 pp., 1930.
58. Bastnagel, Rev. Clement Vincent, J.U.D., The Appointment of Parochial Adjutants and Assistants, XV-257 pp., 1930.
59. Ferry, Rev. William A., A.B., J.C.D., Stole Fees, V-136 pp., 1930.
60. Costello, Rev. John Michael, A.B., J.C.D., Domicile and Quasi-Domicile, VII-201 pp., 1930.

61. Kremer, Rev. Michael Nicholas, A.B., S.T.B., J.C.D., Church Support in the United States, VI-136 pp., 1930.
62. Angula, Rev. Luis, C.M., J.C.D., Legislation de la Iglesia sobre la intencion en la application de la Santa Misa, VII-104 pp., 1931.
63. Frey, Rev. Wolfgang Norbert, O.S.B., A.B., J.C.D., The Act of Religious Profession, VIII-174 pp., 1931.
64. Roberts, Rev. James Brendan, A.B., J.C.D., The Banns of Marriage, XIV-140 pp., 1931.
65. Ryder, Rev. Raymond Aloysius, A.B., J.C.D., Simony, IX-151 pp., 1931.
66. Campagna, Rev. Angelo, Ph.D., J.U.D., Il Vicario Generale del Vescovo, VII-205 pp., 1931.
67. Cox, Rev. Joseph Godfrey, A.B., J.C.D., The Administration of Seminaries, VI-124 pp., 1931.
68. Gregory, Rev. Donald J., J.U.D., The Pauline Privilege, XV-165 pp., 1931.
69. Donohue, Rev. John F., J.C.D., The Impediment of Crime, VII-110 pp., 1931.
70. Dooley, Rev. Eugene A., O.M.I., J.C.D., Church Law on Sacred Relics, IX-143 pp., 1931.
71. Orth, Rev. Clement Raymond, O.M.C., J.C.D., The Approbation of Religious Institutes, 171 pp., 1931.
72. Pernicone, Rev. Joseph M., A.B., J.C.D., The Ecclesiastical Prohibition of Books, XII-267 pp., 1932.
73. Clinton, Rev. Connell, A.B., J.C.D., The Paschal Precept, IX-108 pp., 1932.
74. Donnelly, Rev. Francis B., A.M., S.T.L., J.C.D., The Diocesan Synod, VIII-125 pp., 1932.
75. Torrente, Rev. Camilo, C.M.F., J.C.D., Las Processiones Sagradas, V-145 pp., 1932.
76. Murphy, Rev. Edwin J., C.PP.S., J.C.D., Suspension Ex Informata Conscientia, XI-122 pp., 1932.
77. MacKenzie, Rev. Eric F., A.M., S.T.L., J.C.D., The Delict of Heresy in its Commission, Penalization, Absolution, VII-124 pp., 1932.
78. Lyons, Rev. Avitus E., S.T.B., J.C.D., The Collegiate Tribunal of First Instance, XI-147 pp., 1932.
79. Connolly, Rev. Thomas A., J.C.D., Appeals, XI-195 pp., 1932.
80. Sangmeister, Rev. Joseph V., A.B., J.C.D., Force and Fear as Precluding Matrimonial Consent, V-211 pp., 1932.
81. Jaeger, Rev. Leo A., A.B., J.C.D., The Administration of Vacant and Quasi-Vacant Episcopal Sees in the United States, IX-229 pp., 1932.
82. Rimlinger, Rev. Herbert T., J.C.D., Error Invalidating Matrimonial Consent, VII-79 pp., 1932.

83. BARRETT, REV. JOHN D. M., S.S., J.C.D., A Comparative Study of the Third Plenary Council of Baltimore and the Code, IX-221 pp., 1932.
84. CARBERRY, REV. JOHN J., PHD., S.T.D., J.C.D., The Juridical Form of Marriage, X-177 pp., 1934.
85. DOLAN, REV. JOHN L., A.B., J.C.D., The Defensor Vinculi, XII-157 pp., 1934.
86. HANNAN, REV. JEROME D., A.M., S.T.D., LL.B., J.C.D., The Canon Law of Wills, IX-517 pp., 1934.
87. LEMIEUX, REV. DELISE A., A.M., J.C.D., The Sentence in Ecclesiastical Procedure, IX-131 pp., 1934.
88. O'ROURKE, REV. JAMES J., A.B., J.C.D., Parish Registers, VII-109 pp., 1934.
89. TIMLIN, REV. BARTHOLOMEW, O.F.M., A.M., J.C.D., Conditional Matrimonial Consent, X-381 pp., 1934.
90. WAHL, REV. FRANCIS X., A.B., J.C.D., The Matrimonial Impediments of Consanguinity and Affinity, VI-125 pp., 1934.
91. WHITE, REV. ROBERT J., A.B., LL.B., S.T.B., J.C.D., Canonical Ante-Nuptial Promises and the Civil Law, VI-152 pp., 1934.
92. HERRERA, REV. ANTONIO PARRA, O.C.D., J.C.D., Legislacion Ecclesiastica sobra el Ayuno y la Abstinencia, XI-191 pp., 1935.
93. KENNEDY, REV. EDWIN J., J.C.D., The Special Matrimonial Process in Cases of Evident Nullity, X-165 pp., 1935.
94. MANNING, REV. JOHN J., A.B., J.C.D., Presumption of Law in Matrimonial Procedure, XI-111 pp., 1935.
95. MOEDER, REV. JOHN M., J.C.D., The Proper Bishop for Ordination and Dimissorial Letters, VII-135 pp., 1935.
96. O'MARA, REV. WILLIAM A., A.B., J.C.D., Canonical Causes for Matrimonial Dispensations, IX-155 pp., 1935.
97. REILLY, REV. PETER, J.C.D., Residence of Pastors, IX-81 pp., 1935.
98. SMITH, REV. MARINER T,. O.P., S.T.Lr., J.C.D., The Penal Law for Religious, VII-169 pp., 1935.
99. WHALEN REV. DONALD W., A.M., J.C.D., The Value of Testimonial Evidence in Matrimonal Procedure, XIII-297 pp., 1935.
100. CLEARY, REV. JOSEPH F., J.C.D., Canonical Limitations on the Alienation of Church Property, VIII-141 pp., 1936.
101. GLYNN, REV. JOHN C., J.C.D., The Promoter of Justice, XX-337 pp., 1936.
102. BRENNAN, REV. JAMES H., S.S., M.A., S.T.B., J.C.D., The Simple Convalidation of Marriage, VI-135 pp., 1937.
103. BRUNINI, REV. JOSEPH BERNARD, J.C.D., The Clerical Obligations of Canons 139 and 142, X-121 pp., 1937.
104. CONNOR, REV. MAURICE, A.B., J.C.D., The Administrative Removal of Pastors, VIII-159 pp., 1937.
105. GUILFOYLE, REV. MERLIN JOSEPH, J.C.D., Custom, XI-144 pp., 1937.

106. Hughes, Rev. James Austin, A.B., A.M., J.C.D., Witnesses in Criminal Trials of Clerics, IX-140 pp., 1937.
107. Jansen, Rev. Raymond J., A.B., S.T.L., J.C.D., Canonical Provisions for Catechetical Instruction, VII-153 pp., 1937.
108. Kealy, Rev. John James, A.B., J.C.D., The Introductory Libellus in Church Court Procedure, XI-121 pp., 1937.
109. McManus, Rev. James Edward, C.SS.R., J.C.D., The Administration of Temporal Goods in Religious Institutes, XVI-196 pp., 1937.
110. Moriarity, Rev. Eugene James, J.C.D., Oaths in Ecclesiastical Courts, X-115 pp., 1937.
111. Rainier, Rev. Eligius George, C.SS.R., J.C.D., Suspension of Clerics, XVII-249 pp., 1937.
112. Reilly, Rev. Thomas F., C.SS.R., J.C.D., Visitation of Religious, VI-195 pp., 1938.
113. Moriarity, Rev. Francis E., C.SS.R., J.C.D., The Extraordinary Absolution from Censures, XV-334 pp., 1938.
114. Connolly, Rev. Nicholas P., J.C.D., The Canonical Erection of Parishes, X-132 pp., 1938.
115. Donovan, Rev. James Joseph, J.C.D., The Pastor's Obligation in Prenuptial Investigation, XII-322 pp., 1938.
116. Harrigan, Rev. Robert J., M.A., S.T.B., J.C.D., The Radical Sanation of Invalid Marriages, VIII-208 pp., 1938.
117. Boffa, Rev. Conrad Humbert, J.C.D., Canonical Provisions for Catholic Schools, VII-211 pp., 1939.
118. Parsons, Rev. Anscar John, O.M.Cap., J.C.D., Canonical Elections, XII-236 pp., 1939.
119. Reilly, Rev. Edward Michael, A.B., J.C.D., The General Norms of Dispensation, XII-156 pp., 1939.
120. Ryan, Rev. Gerald Aloysius, A.B., J.C.D., Principles of Episcopal Jurisdiction, XII-172 pp., 1939.
121. Burton, Rev. Francis James, C.S.C., A.B., J.C.D., A Commentary on Canon 1125, X-222 pp., 1940.
122. Miaskiewicz, Rev. Francis Sigismund, J.C.D., Supplied Jurisdiction According to Canon 209, XII-340 pp., 1940.
123. Rice, Rev. Patrick William, A.B., J.C.D., Proof of Death in Prenuptial Investigation, VIII-156 pp., 1940.
124. Anglin, Rev. Thomas Francis, M.S., J.C.D., The Eucharistic Fast, VIII-183 pp., 1941.
125. Coleman, Rev. John Jerome, J.C.D., The Minister of Confirmation, VI-153 pp., 1941.
126. Downs, Rev. John Emmanuel, A.B., J.C.D., The Concept of Clerical Immunity, XI-163 pp., 1941.
127. Esswein, Rev. Anthony Albert, J.C.D., Extrajudicial Penal Powers of Ecclesiastical Superiors, X-144 pp., 1941.

128. FARREL, REV. BENJAMIN FRANCIS, M.A., S.T.L., J.C.D., The Rights and Duties of the Local Ordinary Regarding Congregations of Women Religious of Pontifical Approval, V-195 pp., 1941.

129. FEENEY, REV. THOMAS JOHN, A.B., S.T.L., J.C.D., Restitutio in Integrum, VI-169 pp., 1941.

130. FINDLEY, REV. STEPHEN WILLIAM, O.S.B., A.B., J.C.D., Canonical Norms Governing the Deposition and Degradation of Clerics, XVII-279 pp., 1941.

131. GOODWINE, REV. JOHN, A.B., S.T.L., J.C.D., The Right of the Church to Acquire Property, VIII-119 pp., 1941.

132. HESTON, REV. EDWARD LOUIS, C.S.C., PHD., S.T.D., J.C.D., The Alienation of Church Property in the United States, XII-222 pp., 1941.

133. HOGAN, REV. JAMES JOHN, A.B., S.T.L., J.C.D., Judicial Advocates and Procurators, XIII-200 pp., 1941.

134. KEALY, REV. THOMAS M., A.B., Litt.B., J.C.D., Dowry of Women Religious, IX-152 pp., 1941.

135. KEENE, REV. MICHAEL JAMES, O.S.B., J.C.D., Religious Ordinaries and Canon 198, V-164 pp., 1942.

136. KERIN, REV. CHARLES A., S.S., M.A., S.T.B., J.C.D., The Privation of Christian Burial, XVI-279 pp., 1941.

137. LOUIS, REV. WILLIAM FRANCIS, M.A., J.C.D., Diocesan Archives, X-101 pp., 1941.

138. MCDEVITT, REV. GILBERT JOSEPH, A.B., J.C.D., Legitimacy and Legitimation, X-247 pp., 1941.

139. MCDONOUGH, REV. THOMAS JOSEPH, A.B., J.C.D., Apostolic Administrators, X-217 pp., 1941.

140. MEIER, REV. CARL ANTHONY, A.B., J.C.D., Penal Administrative Procedure Against Negligent Pastors, XI-240 pp., 1941.

141. SCHMIDT, REV. JOHN ROGG, A.B., J.C.D., The Principles of Authentic Interpretation in Canon 17 of the Code of Canon Law, XII-331 pp., 1941.

142. SLAFKOSKY, REV. ANDREW LEONARD, A.B., J.C.D., The Canonical Episcopal Visitation of the Diocese, X-197 pp., 1941.

143. SWOBODA, REV. INNOCENT ROBERT, O.F.M., J.C.D., Ignorance in Relation to the Imputability of Delicts, IX-271 pp., 1941.

144. DUBÉ, REV. ARTHUR JOSEPH, A.B., J.C.D., The General Principles for the Reckoning of Time in Canon Law, VIII-299 pp., 1941.

145. MCBRIDE, REV. JAMES T., A.B., J.C.D., Incardination and Excardination of Seculars, XX-585 pp., 1941.

146. KRÓL, REV. JOHN T., J.C.D., The Defendant in Ecclesiastical Trials, XII-207 pp., 1942.

147. COMYNS, REV. JOSEPH J., C.SS.R., A.B., J.C.D., Papal and Episcopal Administration of Church Property, XIV-155 pp., 1942.

148. Barry, Rev. Garrett Francis, O.M.I., J.C.D., Violation of the Cloister, XII-260 pp., 1942.
149. Bolduc, Rev. Gatien, C.S.V., A.B., S.T.L., J.C.D., Les Études dans les Religions Clèricales, VIII-155 pp., 1942.
150. Boyle, Rev. David John, M.A., J.C.D., The Juridic Effects of Moral Certitude on Pre-Nuptial Guarantees, XII-188 pp., 1942.
151. Canavan, Rev. Walter Joseph, M.A., Litt.D., J.C.D., The Profession of Faith, XII-143 pp., 1942.
152. Desrochers; Rev. Bruno, A.B., Ph.L., S.T.B., J.C.D., Le Premier Concile Plènier de Quebéc et le Code de Droit Canonique, XIV-186 pp., 1942.
153. Dillon, Rev. Robert Edward, A.B., J.C.D., Common Law Marriage, X-148 pp., 1942.
154. Dodwell, Rev. Edward John, Ph.D., S.T.B., J.C.D., The Time and Place for the Celebration of Marriage, X-156 pp., 1942.
155. Donnellan, Rev. Thomas Andrew, A.B., J.C.D., The Obligation of the Missa pro Populo, VII-131 pp., 1942.
156. Eltz, Rev. Louis Anthony, A.B., J.C.L., Cooperation in Crime.
157. Gass, Rev. Sylvester Francis, M.A., J.C.D., Ecclesiastical Pensions, XI-206 pp., 1942.
158. Guiniven, Rev. John Joseph, C.SS.R., J.C.D., The Precept of Hearing Mass, XIV-188 pp., 1942.
159. Gulczynski, Rev. John Theophilus, J.C.D., The Desecration and Violation of Churches, X-126 pp., 1942.
160. Hammil, Rev. John Leo, M.A., J.C.D., The Obligations of the Traveler According to Canon 14, VIII-204 pp., 1942.
161. Haydt, Rev. John Joseph, A.B., J.C.D., Reserved Benefices, XI-148 pp., 1942.
162. Huser, Rev. Roger John, O.F.M., A.B., J.C.D., The Crime of Abortion in Canon Law, XII-187 pp., 1942.
163. Kearney, Rev. Francis Patrick, A.B., S.T.L., J.C.L., The Principles of Canon 1127.
164. Linahen, Rev. Leo James, S.T.L., J.C.D., De Absolutione Complicis In Peccato Turpi, 114 pp., 1942.
165. McCloskey, Rev. Joseph Aloysius, A.B., J.C.D., The Subject of Ecclesiastical Law According to Canon 12, XVII-246 pp., 1942.
166. O'Neil, Rev. Francis Joseph, C.SS.R., J.C.D., The Dismissal of Religious in Temporary Vows, XIII-220 pp., 1942.
167. Prince, Rev. John Edward, A.B., S.T.B., J.C.D., The Diocesan Chancellor, X-136 pp., 1942.
168. Riesner, Rev. Albert Joseph, C.SS.R., J.C.D., Apostates and Fugitives from Religious Institutes, IX-168 pp., 1942.
169. Stenger, Rev. Joseph Bernard, J.C.D., The Mortgaging of Church Property, 186 pp., 1942.

170. WALDRON, REV. JOSEPH FRANCIS, A.B., J.C.D., The Minister of Baptism, XII-197 pp., 1942.
171. WILLETT, REV. ROBERT ALBERT, J.C.D., The Probative Value of Documents in Ecclesiastical Trials, X-124 pp., 1942.
172. WOEBER, REV. EDWARD MARTIN, M.A., J.C.D., The Interpollations, XII-161 pp., 1942.
173. BENKO, REV. MATTHEW ALOYSIUS, O.S.B., M.A., J.C.D., The Abbot *Nullius*, XV-147 pp., 1943.
174. CHRIST, REV. JOSEPH JAMES, M.A., S.T.L., J.C.D., Dispensation from Vindicative Penalties, XIII-285 pp., 1943.
175. CLANCY, REV. PATRICK M. J., O.P., A.B., S.T.LR., J.C.D., The Local Religious Superior, X-229 pp., 1943.
176. CLARKE, REV. THOMAS JAMES, J.C.D., Parish Societies, XII-147 pp., 1943.
177. CONNOLLY, REV. JOHN PATRICK, S.T.L., J.C.D., Synodal Examiners and Parish Priest Consultors, X-223 pp., 1943.
178. DRUMM, REV. WILLIAM MARTIN, A.B., J.C.L., Hospital Chaplains.
179. FLANAGAN, REV. BERNARD JOSEPH, A.B., S.T.L., J.C.D., The Canonical Erection of Religious Houses, X-147 pp., 1943.
180. KELLEHER, REV. STEPHEN JOSEPH, A.B., S.T.B., J.C.D., Discussions with non-Catholics: Canonical Legislation, X-93 pp., 1943.
181. LEWIS, REV. GORDIAN, C.P., J.C.D., Chapters in Religious Institutes, XII-169 pp., 1943.
182. MARX, REV. ADOLPH, J.C.D., The Declaration of Nullity of Marriages Contracted Outside the Church, X-151 pp., 1943.
183. MATULENAS, REV. RAYMOND ANTHONY, O.S.B., A.B., J.C.L., Communication, a Source of Privileges.
184. O'LEARY, REV. CHARLES GERARD, C.SS.R., J.C.D., Religious Dismissed After Perpetual Profession, X-213 pp., 1943.
185. POWER, REV. CORNELIUS MICHAEL, J.C.L., The Blessing of Cemeteries.
186. SHUHLER, REV. RALPH VINCENT, O.S.A., J.C.D., Privileges of Religious to Absolve and Dispense, XII-195 pp., 1943.
187. ZIOLKOWSKI, REV. THADDEUS STANISLAUS, A.B., J.C.D., The Consecration and Blessing of Churches, XII-151 pp., 1943.
188. HENEGHAN, REV. JOHN JOSEPH, S.T.D., J.C.D., The Marriages of Unworthy Catholics: Canons 1065 and 1066.
189. CARROLL, REV. COLEMAN FRANCIS, M.A., S.T.L., J.C.L., Charitable Institutions.
190. CIESLUK, REV. JOSEPH EDWARD, PH.B., S.T.L., J.C.L., National Parishes in the United States.
191. COBURN, REV. VINCENT PAUL, A.B., J.C.L., Marriages of Conscience.
192. CONNORS, REV. CHARLES PAUL, C.S.SP., A.B., J.C.L., Extra-Judicial Procurators in the Code of Canon Law.
193. COYLE, REV. PAUL RAYMOND, A.B., J.C.L., Judicial Exceptions.

194. Fair, Rev. Bartholomew Francis, A.B., S.T.L., J.C.L., The Impediment of Abduction.
195. Gallagher, Rev. Thomas Raphael, O.P., A.B., S.T.Lr., J.C.L., The Examination of the Qualities of the Ordinand.
196. Gannon, Rev. John Mark, S.T.L., J.C.L., The Interstices Required for the Promotion to Orders.
197. Goldsmith, Rev. J. William, B.C.S., S.T.L., J.C.L., The Competence of Church and State over Marriage—Disputed Points.
198. Goodwine, Rev. Joseph Gerard, A.B., S.T.B., J.C.L., The Reception of Converts.
199. Kowalski, Rev. Romuald Eugene, O.F.M., A.B., J.C.L., Sustenance of Religious Houses of Regulars.
200. McCoy, Rev. Alan Edward, O.F.M., J.C.L., Force and Fear in Relation to Delictual Imputability and Penal Responsibility.
201. McDevitt, Rev. Vincent John, Ph.B., S.T.L., J.C.L., Perjury.
202. Martin, Rev. Thomas Owen, Ph.D., S.T.D., J.C.L., Adverse Possession, Prescription and Limitation of Actions: The Canonical "Praescriptio."
203. Miklosovic, Rev. Paul John, A.B., J.C.L., Attempted Marriages and Their Consequent Juridic Effects.
204. Mundy, Rev. Thomas Maurice, A.B., S.T.L., J.C.L., The Union of Parishes.
205. O'Day, Rev. John Coyle, A.B., J.C.L., The Matrimonial Impediment of Nonage.
206. Olalia, Rev. Alexander Ayson, S.T.L., J.C.L., A Comparative Study of the Christian Constitution of States and the Constitution of the Philippine Commonwealth.
207. Poisson, Rev. Pierre-Marie, C.S.C., A.B., Ph.L., ThL., J.C.L., Droits Patrimoniaux des Maisons et des Églises Religieuses.
208. Stadalnikas, Rev. Casimir Joseph, M.I.C., J.C.L., Reservation of Censures.
209. Sullivan, Rev. Eugene Henry, S.T.L., J.C.L., Proof of the Reception of the Sacraments.
210. Vaughan, Rev. William Edward, J.C.L., Constitutions for Diocesan Courts.
211. Lyons, Rev. Joseph Henry, J.C.L., The Joinder of Issue in Canonical Trials.

www.ingramcontent.com/pod-product-compliance
Lightning Source LLC
LaVergne TN
LVHW050229080826
844660LV00012B/500

9780813223889